THE
Serenity Prayer
BOOK

THE
Serenity
Prayer
BOOK

William V. Pietsch

HarperSanFrancisco
A Division of HarperCollins*Publishers*

FIRST EDITION

Library of Congress Cataloging-in-Publication Data

Pietsch, William V.
    The serenity prayer book / William V. Pietsch. — 1st ed.
      p.   cm.
    ISBN 0-06-250682-X (alk. paper)
    1. Prayers. I. Title.
BV284.S47P54   1990   89-46441
242'.726 — dc20   CIP

91 92 93 94 K.P. 10 9 8 7 6 5 4 3 2

This edition is printed on acid-free paper that meets the American National Standards Institute Z39.48 Standard.

Dedicated
in loving memory
of
my father and mother
and sister

Table of Contents

Acknowledgments

I am grateful to many people for their thoughts and insights in the writing of this book.

In my understanding of prayer and the problems of suffering, I have found the books of Harry Emerson Fosdick to be particularly helpful. Other writers, among many, who have enriched my perspective in life are Carl Jung, C. S. Lewis, Eric Neumann, Reinhold Niebuhr, Pierre Teilhard de Chardin, and Bill W.

In the preparation of this book I appreciate the encouragement and suggestions of my son Jim Pietsch, my daughter Patti Pietsch-Wise, and my son-in-law, Mark Wise.

I am also grateful for those who have read sections of the manuscript and responded with comments, especially Barbara Adams, Tom Cunningham, Jim Lambert, Doug Lind, William Parsons, Terry Reed, Lucy Sharp, and Susan and George West.

I appreciate the support of a group of friends with whom I have met regularly in sharing and prayer: Steve Baer, Peter Baiardi, Briggs Baugh, Bill Boyd, Kim Chaffee, Gary Cosgrave, Len Freas, Charlie Hasser, Drew Jones, Jon Kent, Les Madorsky, and George Miller.

Special thanks to Buz Wyeth for his initial interest in the manuscript and his practical help.

In the physical preparation of the manuscript, I am grateful to Renée Moore, Joan Gibbs, and Betsy Reis for their help in typing, and to Jerry Davidoff and Stan Drake for the use of their copy machines.

I am very grateful for the help of Barbara Moulton of Harper & Row for her enthusiasm, patience, and sensitivity in editing. I would also like to thank Barbara Archer for her efficient attention to details as the editorial assistant. Thanks also to copy editor Priscilla Stuckey-Kauffman and production editor Mimi Kusch for their valuable help.

And, most importantly, I want to express deep appreciation to my wife, the Reverend Dr. Louise Parsons Pietsch — "Weezie" — for her continuous support throughout the writing, for her theological insights, for her steady loving care, and for the inspiration of her faith.

W. V. P.

THE
Serenity
Prayer
BOOK

Introduction

When I mentioned to someone I knew that I was writing a book about the Serenity Prayer, he replied, "The Serenity Prayer? That's a prayer I say every day of my life!"

He is not alone. In periods of crisis many people turn to these words for strength and insight. In fact, the Serenity Prayer is one of the most widely circulated prayers of all time. Printed in a variety of forms, millions of copies have been distributed throughout the world.

In recent years it has become increasingly well known and used, especially by people in programs of recovery from alcoholism and other addictions. Alcoholics Anonymous has included it in its literature, and its familiar words are often found in billfolds nestled among credit cards or next to a driver's license.

But why a book about these familiar words? Aren't they already clear and understandable?

They are. But sometimes we can be surprised by the familiar. A well-known phrase we have heard again and again can suddenly take on a deeper meaning: "I thought I knew what 'one day at a time' meant. Now I *really* see what it means." And later on those same words can take on an even deeper meaning.

One of the purposes of this book is to help see something familiar in new and different ways.

Familiar words can sometimes numb us to their meaning. You may have had the experience I have had with this prayer. Sometimes I just say the first few words and the rest then follow automatically. While it seems like praying, I know that this automatic replay is not real prayer because my feelings and my thoughts are not present with the words. Clearly, just saying isn't the same as praying.

If one of the values of prayer is its ability to change our perspective, simply reciting words will not do much for us. Thinking clearly about the meaning of each word as we say it — and participating in that meaning — is the path toward growth.

The purpose of this book is to deepen understanding of the Serenity Prayer so that you will experience more serenity, more courage, and more wisdom in your life. To help in understanding its meaning, the book has been divided into chapters that explore the words and phrases in the order they occur:

1. *God*
2. *Grant me*
3. *Serenity*
4. *To accept the things I cannot change*
5. *Courage*
6. *To change the things I can*
   and
7. *Wisdom to know the difference*

You may prefer to read only certain sections or read the chapters in a different order; however, the value in seeing the prayer as a whole is a fuller understanding of its power and insight.

1
God

G*od*, the very first word in
the prayer, raises questions in the minds of many people,
perhaps in most of us.

Yet if we are to pray the prayer at all we need some
sort of understanding of what or who God is.

For some people, an understanding of God is not a
problem: "It's obvious!" For me, and I'm sure for some
others, belief is not that simple. In fact, the more I think
about God, the more complicated it becomes. Perhaps
some of those who accept trust in God so quickly are
just closing their eyes to areas of life that might complicate their beliefs.

I once heard someone say, "Religious people aren't
very thoughtful, and thoughtful people aren't very reli-

gious." When I first heard that statement, it seemed quite true. Yet since then I have met a growing number of people who are both religious, in the best sense of that word, and very thoughtful as well.

What do they believe about God? Or, to be more specific, how can I, as a thoughtful person, understand God?

What I need is some sort of understanding that does not require me to deny some of the realities I see in the world around me. I see examples of suffering and injustice that the simple words *have faith* just don't solve.

It is not that I have to have all the answers before I can have any kind of trust. In a lot of areas of life I trust even though my knowledge is incomplete. For example, when I drive my car to the airport and get on a plane I trust myself to the care of the pilot without much information about him or her as a person. But my trust is not unreasonable. At least, I am not expected to accept things about the pilot that are contrary to my best thinking.

Some religious claims, however, seem inconsistent with what my mind tells me is true. I have to weigh what religious authorities say with other experiences in life, and sometimes the two just do not match. No matter how much I am told that I *ought* to believe in someone else's concept of God, unless it makes sense deep within myself

{ 5 }

I cannot accept it. The only God that I can have a relationship with is one consistent with my own thoughts when I am thinking most clearly.

For example, I have found it difficult to accept without question the concept that God is all-powerful and all-loving. When I first heard that description it raised some problems for me. If God is so powerful and loving, why are there so many tragedies in the world? Perhaps God is loving but not powerful or powerful but not loving. I could not see how it could be both ways.

Yet there are people, thoughtful people, who have faced deep personal suffering, whose definition of God still includes the words *powerful* and *loving.*

Evidently different ways of understanding God are possible. And what I need is a definition so large that I will not have to discard it as I become more and more aware of the world around me.

Some descriptions of God are so limiting that when I have tried to fit them with my personal experience I have been greatly disappointed.

In *The Color Purple,* author Alice Walker uses these words to express the feelings of one of her characters, a black woman: "When I found out I thought God was white, and a man, I lost interest."* This comment illus-

*Alice Walker, *The Color Purple* (Simon & Schuster, 1985), p. 202.

trates what is generally true for most of us: *The way we think about God ultimately affects how we relate to God.*

On August 6, 1961, Russian cosmonaut Gherman Titov began the first extended journey through space, circling the earth more than seventeen times. While passing over Japan he received a radio message that was evidently meant for him.

"It was in very bad Russian," he laughed, telling about it later, "but I could make out quite clearly that it was directed to me. They — on the ground — were talking about God and of angels and of the heavens. I looked through the window of the spaceship and thought if there was a God here I couldn't see him."*

Ideas of God from past generations, such as a humanlike figure up in the sky, no longer make sense for a great many people. Scientific research in areas such as astronomy and psychology has radically changed how we see our world and ourselves. This changed perspective has inevitably influenced our thought about God — and our relationship with God as well.

Someone once defined superstition as "giving religious significance to our ignorance." A lot of ideas about God do grow out of ignorance. Yet it is also true that some people have given a great deal of thought to what it

*Gherman Titov, *I Am Eagle!* (Indianapolis, IN: Bobbs-Merrill, 1962), p. 16.

means to relate to God. Theology has been called the science of God — from *theos,* the Greek word for God. The central concern of such theology, both past and present, is to think clearly about God.

For some people, however, this kind of thinking raises other questions.

The theologian C. S. Lewis tells of an experience he once had while giving a talk about his understanding of God. A member of the audience stood up afterward and said, "I've no use for all that stuff. But, mind you, I'm a religious man too. I *know* there's a God. I've *felt* him — out alone in the desert at night, the tremendous mystery. And that's just why I don't believe all your neat little dogmas and formulas about him. To anyone who's met the real thing they all seem so petty and pedantic and unreal!"

Lewis replied that he agreed with the man. There is a difference, he said, between an experience of God and saying something about God. Talking *about* God can be a turning from something real to something less real, like looking at the Atlantic Ocean from the beach and then turning to look at a map of the Atlantic. It means going from real waves to colored paper. Yet the map is based on what hundreds and thousands of people have found out about that ocean. "It has behind it masses of experiences just as real as the one you could have from the beach, only while yours would be a single isolated glimpse, the map fits all those isolated experiences together. . . . Doctrines are not God: they are only a kind of map."*

The author of the Serenity Prayer is a person who not only has studied what others have thought about God but also has constantly sought to relate his own experience to such learning. To understand the prayer, it might be useful to know something about the person who wrote it and how he thought about God from his own experience and study.

Reinhold Niebuhr is considered to be the author of the prayer, although he may have drawn on previous sources. He was on the faculty of Union Theological Seminary in New York for many years, and occasionally he preached in a small church near his summer home in Heath, Massachusetts. After Niebuhr used the prayer in a worship service at the church in 1934, Harold Chandler Robbins, a summer neighbor, asked for a copy. Niebuhr reportedly handed him the original with words such as, "Here, take the prayer. I have no further use for it."

His original wording was:

O God, give us
> *serenity to accept what cannot be changed*
> *courage to change what should be changed*
> *and wisdom to distinguish the one from the other.*

*C. S. Lewis, *Mere Christianity* (New York: Macmillan, 1952), p. 136.

{ 9 }

Robbins, the neighbor, printed it in a pamphlet the following year. It was later published in newspapers and included in literature by Alcoholics Anonymous and other groups.

One of the values of this prayer is the way in which it enriches our understanding of God. Each phrase implies something about who God is and what it means to have a relationship with a Higher Power.

Niebuhr's approach to understanding God is useful because it is based not on some vague abstract concept but on the human *experience* of God in the concrete world in which we live.

At the heart of Niebuhr's faith is the belief that the way we understand God directly affects the way we understand ourselves and the actions we take in life.

It is not uncommon to find people making important changes based on their understanding of God. Sometimes belief relates to a moral decision. Some make decisions out of fear of punishment from God, others out of a response to what they see as God's love. Some see terrorism as a fulfillment of God's will and look forward to a reward from God for martyrdom. Taking a courageous stand on an unpopular issue may be related directly to an understanding of God's will. Actions, both positive and negative, can be greatly affected by a person's belief in God.

Some people, however, think that belief in God has little or no effect on their actions. They see themselves as primarily neutral about such matters.

A common notion is that people either have a response to God or they do not. Actually it is not that simple. Once the word *God* has been used, everyone who reads — or hears — the word is affected in some way. No one can be completely neutral. There will always be some sort of connection or response to whatever the word *God* means to each person.

One person may experience puzzlement, for another it may be peace, for another it may be anger, gratitude, fear, or something else. Once God is named, a response of some sort occurs toward whatever comes to mind when the word *God* is spoken.

And the quality or character of our response is determined by our definition of God. Even if we define God as "not there," we are still experiencing some response. A child with an absent parent is never completely neutral about the situation. If some children have fathers and you do not, you experience some response to the word *father*. Saying, "It doesn't matter to me at all," may not quite ring true. Emotionally, the situation has some effect on you, if only a vague uncertainty deep within. People who say that belief in God does not matter at all often secretly live with a feeling of uncertainty about it.

We cannot deliberately reject something without defining what we are rejecting. The question is not, "*Does* God have a meaning for me?" but, "What *kind* of meaning does God have?"

Some definitions of God are better than others. At least, some definitions are clearly more acceptable than others; some definitions fit better with what seems true within us.

To develop a trusting relationship with God requires some risk taking on our parts, a willingness to explore seriously our own understanding of what God means to us.

Probably the major barrier to growth that we face as human beings is our tendency to hold tight to what is familiar. The primary purpose of psychotherapy is, in fact, to help people recognize which patterns, perhaps useful in the past, may not necessarily be appropriate in the present.

One of the greatest contributions of Reinhold Niebuhr was his challenge to fixed and rigid positions people held about religion. He was especially critical of church members who were piously optimistic about their own moral goodness. He once put it this way: "If there were a drunken orgy somewhere, I would bet ten to one a church member was not in it. But if there were a lynching, I would bet ten to one a church member was in it."*

Over and over Niebuhr challenged the self-righteousness of those in the church who used belief in God to arrogantly justify their actions.

Niebuhr also pointed out, however, that while some in the church protect themselves by closing their minds, some outside the church are also not open to new knowledge. Some people reject all contact with religion because of childish ideas about God — concepts that thoughtful people have long since outgrown.

A tendency is widespread today to assume in the name of tolerance that all beliefs are of equal value, that it is a sign of prejudice to state that any viewpoint in life is better than another.

Yet the word *prejudice* means "to pre-judge," to jump to conclusions about something without really examining it. Tolerance does not require believing that all statements about something are of equal value and equally true. To have respect for another person is not the same as agreeing with the other's viewpoint no matter what it may be.

*Quoted by Jane Bingham in *Courage to Change* (New York: Scribner, 1972), p. 147.

If we are to have a clear understanding of who God is and who we are, one of the first requirements is a willingness to explore what thoughtful people say about their relationship with God, without pre-judging it.

In the Serenity Prayer Niebuhr expresses thoughts and feelings about God that were a part of his life and career over a period of years. While the original prayer contains only twenty-seven words, and the simplified version even fewer, it is important to note that the perspective presented in the prayer is not casual. It emerges out of many years of experience and thought.

Even though Niebuhr's viewpoint may not completely fit with our own, we may still find it useful to stand where he stood and to look at the world from his perspective. Whether another viewpoint is the same or in contrast with our own, sharing in another's experience, strength, and hope can often help us to see our own experience more clearly.

Each of the following chapters expands on what has been said about God in this chapter. As we explore the rest of the words and phrases of the Serenity Prayer, it will be useful to keep returning to your own thought and experience as the basis of belief, and to keep asking, "How does the perspective in this prayer fit in with my own understanding of God and myself?"

2
Grant Me

The two words *grant me* speak about a very specific way of understanding God. They indicate that in some way God can give us something. This concept is in contrast with a religious view that God is "everything," including ourselves. It says instead that God is "Other" — some Being that we can relate to and receive from.

Yet what *can* we receive from God if we do ask?

Disappointment with what they receive or do not receive when they pray is one of the main reasons people give for not believing in God. I remember someone telling me once, somewhat humorously, about the lack of response he felt in prayer. "Couldn't God, if he were there, do *something*? at least say 'Hi'? All I get is silence."

Well, what does God give us when we pray? The Serenity Prayer indicates that it is something *within*: serenity, courage, wisdom.

A major problem that occurs with prayer is that it can be confused with working and thinking. We sometimes expect from prayer results that come instead through action or thought.

Let us clarify which topics are and are not appropriate for prayer. Generally we should not expect God to do for us those things that obviously are not related to the purpose of prayer. For instance, when our car gets a flat tire we do not expect to replace it through the power of prayer; that is an area for work. Also, we use thinking, not praying, to add a column of figures. Yet, as apparent as this may be in these simplistic illustrations, sometimes we may be disappointed when God does not miraculously solve problems that require thought or work to accomplish.

While at times the areas of working, thinking, and praying may overlap, we are less likely to experience disappointment if we can separate the three functions at least in our minds.

Praying is basically a way of changing what we are experiencing within ourselves. It has to do with peacefulness within, strength and insight for both ourselves and others. (More about others later; see chapter 6.)

Yet the question keeps coming up, "To what or whom are our prayers being directed?"

I once asked a minister for his definition of God. His answer was, "The feeling of a Presence." While I could not deny that answer as a possibility, I did not find it particularly helpful.

Years later I came across another description of God: not simply "a Presence" — but the Empowering Presence.

Again, while such a definition did not say enough about God, the idea of God as empowering fit with what I observed to be true in the lives of some people — people who had been changed in very positive ways. The source of these changes, they said, was "the Higher Power," an Empowering Presence that was available for those who needed strength and insight.

Were these people simply deluding themselves? Did they believe because such belief was easier than facing reality?

As a psychotherapist whose job it is to help people move toward emotional health, I had to ask the question, "How healthy *are* these people who are turning to a Higher Power for meaning for their lives?" Instead of finding persons who were increasingly weak and dependent, I found that the opposite was true. They were, instead, moving toward a new strength and maturity.

But what defines psychological maturity? For me, the first characteristic is *an ability to face reality,* not to pretend or avoid facing those difficulties that occur in life, such as an impending loss of a job, the death of a close friend, or facing something we don't like in ourselves. When we have personal difficulties our first tendency is often denial. Psychologically there seems to be a protective mechanism within us to keep us from feeling overwhelmed. The psychologically healthy person, however, is one who, instead of living in continuous denial, faces the reality and goes on. Instead of hiding away in an imaginary world, the healthy person moves away from denial and toward a risking of awareness.

The second characteristic of a healthy person, as I see it, is *the ability to relate well with other people.* This ability to relate well means something far deeper than acting pleasant toward others. It has to do with actually feeling less critical of them. Psychologically healthy people do not constantly feel mad at the world. Having faced character defects within themselves and accepted those defects, they actually *feel* less anger toward others. Healthy people, by seeing themselves more clearly, are more willing to make amends to those they have injured, even when it is difficult.

The third characteristic of a healthy person has already been mentioned. It is *a willingness to be honest with ourselves.* One of the greatest problems we face is what psychology defines as rationalization — using reason to deny certain facts about the world and who we are. While for some people religion has been a means of rationalizing, for others a relationship with a Higher Power has made it possible to risk a greater awareness of the world and their part in it.

Among those who have felt an Empowering Presence in their lives, I have been particularly impressed by some who have found a new life after they had hit bottom because of drugs or alcohol. Many whose lives had become unmanageable found a relationship with God as the way to a new maturity.

Some who were psychologically most healthy were people who had actively participated in a spiritual program of recovery from addiction. Those who were involved in this program over a period of years seemed to have a special quality of life in facing problems of living and an honesty about themselves as well.

This recovery program, which includes twelve steps, began some fifty years ago and was intended, at the beginning, for those addicted to alcohol. Under the name Alcoholics Anonymous, it has now become the most effective method *by far* for recovery from alcoholism. Because of its tremendous success, it has been used as a model for other programs of recovery as well in such areas as gambling, cocaine, even overeating.

Perhaps the most startling results I saw from the program were the changes in the lives of those who participated. These changes began at a point of desperation. Their lives had become unmanageable. Intelligent, even brilliant, people, no matter how hard they tried, could not overcome their difficulties. Some had lost their friends or their family; others had lost their health, their money, or their job. Still others had lost all of these things. Some had hit bottom farther down than others, but each had reached a point where life had closed in on them and they saw no way out.

How did the change occur?

The answer was ultimately found in *a Power beyond themselves.*

While it is often assumed that self-confidence is the bottom line in moving ahead in life, as a psychotherapist I was faced with the fact that, among the most psychologically healthy people I saw, the starting point was not self-confidence but the opposite. They had found new life, *not* through more faith in their own ability, but *through less faith in their own power and more faith in a Power greater than themselves.*

The more I saw these people, the more intrigued I became. What impressed me most was a depth of life

{ 20 }

and an ease of living that is seldom seen. They seemed to define what it means to be human in the best sense of the word.

In a book about the history of Alcoholics Anonymous, Ernest Kurtz points out that such humanness comes from an insight that, for many, seems alien to American thought: "*To be human* was first to be *not God*, to be other than omnipotent or absolutely autonomous."*

The basic book about the program, *Alcoholics Anonymous*, puts it succinctly in these few words: "First of all, we had to quit playing God."

Here, it seemed, was strong empirical evidence that recognition of a Power greater than ourselves can change human lives in a profound and positive way.

Some might question whether a so-called spiritual way of life made much practical difference. Here, however, there could be little doubt in terms of *results*. Those who had been leading the most destructive of lives not only recovered from addiction, but went on from there to a deeper maturity and greater understanding of life than most people I knew.

Grant me are two words that, in spite of their simplicity, describe a profound perspective in life, a perspective that has been called "the beginning of wisdom."

---

*Ernest Kurtz, *Not-God: A History of Alcoholics Anonymous* (Center City, MN: Hazelden, 1979), p. 196 (italics added).

These two words acknowledge that we as humans are not the center of the universe. There is an "Other." Or, as someone once described it, the practical implication of belief in a Higher Power is, "I am not *it*."

In response to someone's difficulty in believing in God, a member of AA once put it this way: "You don't have to believe in God to be a part of the program. All you have to believe is that *you* are *not God!*"

In essence, this seems to be the critical turning point that leads to the new life of maturity.

As humans we seem to live in an area between two dangerous extremes: despair and arrogance. Without a belief in some Power beyond ourselves, we may fall into despair, feeling that ultimately all depends on us, and we do not have the strength or insight to fix things.

Or, at the other extreme, without a belief in some Power beyond ourselves we may fall into arrogance, an attitude we hate in other people but seldom see in ourselves. How easy it is, when we are not feeling good about ourselves, to slip into criticizing others! While religion can be, and sometimes is, used to justify criticism of others, an honest look at ourselves in the light of what we see as God's intentions for us can bring us back to reality — and a sense of humility.

Sometimes religion is described as wishful thinking. In fact, it can be just the opposite. A relationship with a

Higher Power, instead of being comfortable coasting, can call us to our highest and best. One of the things that convinces me most of the existence of God in my life is that I am moved to do those things that I may not want to do but that are ultimately for my highest good — and are a true fulfillment of my self.

Yet if there is a Higher Power working for our best, why is it necessary to *ask* for things? Is God so reluctant to give that we have to beg for what is good for us?

The words *grant me* refer not to changing God so that God will give, but rather changing ourselves so that we can receive.

One of the most frustrating problems that friends and relatives face with an addicted person is the attitude of denial that a difficulty even exists: "That's ridiculous! I don't have a problem! I can stop anytime I want!" Help and concern may be there waiting, but until the person sees his or her need of help nothing much happens. The beginning of change occurs, however, at the point where the words *Help me* are spoken sincerely. The attitude expressed in those words is the turning point toward recovery.

The words *grant me* help create an attitude within ourselves that makes receiving possible.

3

Serenity

Т he young man in my office
took off his glasses and wiped his eyes, first with his sleeve
and then with his hand. He looked at me knowingly. Jim
and I had talked about Sue many times.* Now the relationship with her was ending. He had feared it would
happen before now. In fact, that concern had been there
when he first came in to see me many months ago. I
recall the desperation in his eyes when we first met. I
remember questioning him about being suicidal.

This time he had a different look about him. I saw
sadness, yes, but not the same sense of helpless futility.
His face showed an inner calmness that had not been
present before. I knew that this time he would meet this
painful situation and eventually work it through.

*All names have been changed to maintain anonymity.

For years, Jim had been heavily into drugs, a great variety of them. After a while he had settled into a pattern of marijuana and alcohol and described himself as "stoned all day, every day." Now it was different; through the Twelve-Step program he had been free for months of all drugs and was sober.

While outwardly Jim was still facing some difficult situations, he had experienced a basic shift in his viewpoint about life. It was more than simply not using drugs; his life had changed profoundly within. He faced the problems before him without the intense anxiety he had known before.

What is significant here is *how* Jim's life was different. Outwardly the circumstances had not changed very much at that point; the situation was still very painful. What was different was what had happened *within*. He experienced less feeling of helplessness and an inner strength he had not known before.

In another session, some weeks later, the inner change in Jim was even more evident when he said, "I just found out I've got fingernails!" In response to my puzzled look, he went on, "All my life I've been biting my fingernails — and now I'm not doing that anymore!"

To him, and to me, it was a sign of how deeply his change in perspective had altered his life. He had not *tried* to stop biting his fingernails, he discovered he had stopped. Something powerful had happened deep within. He found a serenity in himself with a depth that surprised him.

To live with serenity does not necessarily mean that outward conditions have changed. *Serenity is an inner peace that is present even in difficult surroundings.*

It is important to note that the serenity Jim found came about in the *presence* of problems, not through a *denial* of them. It was peace that grew from inner depth, not a quick cure that gave the impression of serenity. False serenity quickly fades and needs constant renewal because it is based on a denial of reality. The way of denial brings serenity through an avoidance of outward conditions — a pretense to ourselves and others that difficulties are not there.

Today, one of the most common ways of denial is chemical pretense, the use of alcohol or drugs to pretend that certain problems are not real. While such hiding from difficulties brings a serenity of sorts, unsolved problems have a way of coming back again — and again — and with them the need to repeat the denial. Needing briefly and repeatedly to satisfy this urge for denial is what is called addiction.

Although we tend to think of addiction as the misuse of drugs, a broader definition includes other methods of denial as well. John Bradshaw, theologian and lecturer, has observed that addiction can include *any kind of mood-altering experience* that has *life-damaging consequences.* It can include substances, relationships, shopping, sex, even religion, if it is basically harmful to ourselves or others. To deliberately choose unawareness, by whatever method, affects not only the person in denial but others as well.

I remember visiting a friend some years ago who worked at a university. Behind the desk in his office was a finely crafted wooden sign with gold letters. It read,

> If everyone is running around wringing their hands and crying, and you are cool, calm, and collected, *you don't understand the situation.*

Unawareness of a situation *can* produce a feeling that some might label serenity. The problem with such serenity, however, is that it is a private serenity that is ultimately destructive to others and ourselves as well.

The person with a gambling, drug, or religious addiction may feel very good within yet be completely unaware of how those actions are deeply hurting the lives of those close by. Instead of recognizing how his or her actions disrupt the serenity of others, the addicted person has a tendency to become secretive about the addiction, not realizing that what seems so secret is clearly evident to others.

This private serenity with limited awareness of what is happening "out there" eventually is affected by those very surroundings. People "out there" respond with frustration to the person in denial, making his or her life so unpleasant that more denial is needed to feel good. The addicted person repeats the cycle again and again, with increasing frustration for all.

True serenity grows not out of an avoidance of reality but through *a seeing and an accepting of the world as it is, balanced with the wisdom and courage to change it,* as we will see in the chapters that follow.

No discussion of serenity would be complete here, however, without a few words about that seeming disturber of serenity called the conscience.

While our serenity can be affected by events in the world, we can sometimes experience even greater pain from within ourselves — that familiar uneasiness that can affect our days and disturb our sleep. What is the relationship between the conscience and our serenity?

Surprisingly, few psychology books refer to the dynamics of the conscience, which is such a basic part of our human nature. Some view the conscience as growing out of a moralistic attitude instilled by overly critical parents. Others see the conscience as the voice of God within us. Actually, it is a psychological mechanism that measures how close we are or how distant we are from what we ourselves know is right.

It is important to note that the conscience does not give us some absolute standard of what is right. It tells us rather about ourselves — how far we have departed from what *we know* is right, how distant we are from our own standard of right and wrong.

The conscience takes its cue from each person's individual knowledge and experience.

In Mark Twain's book *Huckleberry Finn* the young boy, Huck, is drifting down a river on a raft with a slave, Jim. Huck's conscience bothers him because he is helping a slave escape. Harriet Tubman, living in about the same time in history as the novel, had a different response from her conscience. A fugitive slave herself, she returned again and again to help free hundreds of others.

The reason for the difference in conscience is that the conscience responds in an individual way to each person's thought and past experiences in life. *The conscience changes as we become more aware of ourselves and our world.* When the mind has more information, the conscience has more data to work on and so responds in different ways as our knowledge grows.

There is a saying in the computer industry: "Garbage in, garbage out." It means that if poor data are fed into a fine computer, what comes out are poor data. The conscience operates in much the same way. If we have grown up in a dysfunctional family the conscience may have limited and confusing data to work with.

Does this mean, then, that the conscience is not reliable — that we shouldn't listen to the voice of the conscience within us?

Actually, it means just the reverse: The conscience is a very sensitive inner gauge that measures — based on the information we have — how far we are from the highest values we know. As we move away from our highest values, pain increases. Pain lessens as we move toward acceptance of our own highest values. Shame, in contrast to conscience, can work as a rejection of our highest self if we feel that blame from others is the final standard of self-worth.

It is not always easy to separate shame, the echo of blame from the past, from the conscience, the inner voice of the self. Help may be needed from caring and perceptive friends or a qualified professional.

The conscience itself, however, is basically very reliable. While it may not always give us what might be termed the best answer, it does give us the best answer available to us based on our own experience and thought.

While at first it may seem that getting rid of the conscience is the way to get inner peace, in reality, *the conscience is a path within that leads us closer and closer to real serenity.*

4

To Accept the Things I Cannot Change

I n thinking about how God answers prayer, it is useful to consider a definition of God that is consistent with the viewpoint of the prayer's author: the concept of God as *Creator.*

This understanding of God contrasts with those who see God as everything, including ourselves. To see God as Creator has a different emphasis, one that helps make sense in sorting out the problems we find in the world around us.

To see God as Creator is to see God not *as* all things but *in* all things. Just as a painter may put a lot of himself or herself into a painting, the painter is not the painting. In the view that sees God as the Creator of the heavens and the earth, God is not simply those things, but "Other."

Although this may seem like splitting hairs theologically, once we take seriously the concept of God as Creator, many things that formerly were puzzling fall into place. The view of God as Creator helps to make sense of our world and helps us see more clearly who we are as human beings.

To take seriously that God is the Creator is both helpful and disturbing. It is helpful in that it explains some of the things about God that previously did not feel right; it is disturbing in that it sees God as limited.

Yet *to create means to set limits.*

As humans we create something by putting limits on whatever object we create. In building a piece of furniture, such as a table, we make it only so long, so wide, and of a certain height. It cannot be infinitely long or wide. We say it stops *here* and goes no farther than *that.* To create is to set limits.

Creating a painting or a piece of music requires putting paint here but not there, using this musical note, not that one. To fulfill our purpose we put limits on what we do — that is the nature of creation.

To understand God as Creator means that God also sets limits in creating — *and those limits that God sets also limit God!*

Sometimes, to make themselves feel better, people sentimentalize what God can do: "God can do everything!" Yet if we take seriously that God is Creator, even God is limited. To create "this" and have it be "not this" at the same time is a contradiction in terms.

From this viewpoint, God in creating sets certain necessary limits for our good, which also can, and do, cause us great difficulties.

For example, a major cause of suffering for human beings is *the creation of dependable laws in nature.* Wood burns, whether in a fireplace or in the walls of a home. That is the nature of wood. We can depend on it. Water, as a substance, does not suddenly and unexpectedly turn itself into sulfuric acid; it follows predictable, dependable laws. If we step too close to the edge of a cliff and fall off we can depend on the fact that gravity will pull us down toward the earth. If we do not learn to fit in with those consistent laws of nature, we can cause great problems for ourselves and sometimes for others as well.

Yet without such reliable laws in nature our world would be without order. In spite of the difficulties we face and the suffering that results, it is useful to live in a world that is basically reliable. The answer to many of our difficulties is not found in moving away from an orderly world but in our learning to accept and fit in with what has been given for our good.

{ 33 }

The great psychiatrist Carl Jung once stated, "Neurosis is always a substitute for legitimate suffering."* What he means by this is that neuroses — the most common problems in emotional and mental health — come about because we are not willing to face legitimate suffering, suffering that follows from those things built into the very character of creation itself.

Legitimate suffering is suffering that comes about because of the necessary order of things. Even as human beings we create a useful orderliness that makes life easier. A simple example of this is our use of traffic lights. Obviously they make life safer and easier, yet they also create frustrations at times for both drivers and pedestrians. Yet however annoying such experiences may be, they are indeed a form of legitimate suffering — necessary because of the order of things.

Someone once described a universal prayer (acceptable to people of many faiths) as, "God, please alter all the laws of the universe to meet my particular need at this time."

One sign of a healthy person is the recognition that order also brings difficulties. Emotionally healthy people do not continually deny the reality of legitimate suffering.

But is all suffering really legitimate? Many things

*C. G. Jung, *Psychology and Religion: West and East* (Princeton Univ. Press, 1969), p. 75.

{ 34 }

that occur in the world seem simply unjust, unfair to innocent people.

While no one has a simple answer to the problems of suffering, two other factors seem worth considering as we face this difficult and complicated question.

One of these factors is *our interconnectedness,* our togetherness.

If one person does not fit in with the dependable laws of nature, this person's actions may injure not only the self but other people as well. Arguments and wars would be drastically reduced if we were all hermits! But interconnectedness is a part of life that most of us would not want eliminated.

Another cause of suffering for both ourselves and others is *our human ability to make choices in life.*

While some people doubt that we as humans have freedom of choice, that we are so conditioned by our environment that we cannot choose, that view does not seem true to life as I know it.

As a psychotherapist, I have seen many people whose choices have been very limited. Circumstances such as living with an illness or in a difficult work situation or with a critical person can bring feelings of futility, with seemingly no choices. Yet I have been surprised to see how choices can be made in situations such as these. Choices do change the circumstances, or if not the circumstances, the way of handling them.

One of the reasons the Serenity Prayer speaks to so many people is because it combines reality with hope. It does not gloss over the fact that we do face certain situations in life that "cannot be changed," yet it goes on to say that choices are possible, that we can make decisions and take actions that make a difference in living. (More about this in chapters 5 and 6.)

We may say we want God to make the world better, without thinking through just what we mean by that. To make a world without dependable laws? To create a world in which each of us is alone and has no effect on others? To have a world where we are mechanical robots without the power of choice?

A world of dependable laws, where we are not alone and where we have the power of choice, is a complicated world. A friend can die in an automobile accident, an innocent baby can be born addicted to heroin.

It is tragic to have such things happen when we lack awareness of what we are doing. It is even more tragic to try to solve the problems we face by deliberately creating unawareness through denial. Whether through chemical pretense or other forms of denial, the result is still the same: Continual avoidance of problems does not solve them.

As previously mentioned, the Serenity Prayer combines reality with hope. Instead of a world in which we grit our teeth and bear it because nothing can be done, this prayer reminds us that *change is possible* as we face our limits, and with courage and wisdom place our hope in an Empowering Presence beyond ourselves.

In thinking about the Empowering Presence, I am reminded of an experience of Martin Luther King, Jr., in one of the most difficult periods of his life when he faced things he could not change.

As he took on leadership of the civil rights movement, he began to receive threatening phone calls and letters. At first he questioned the seriousness of such threats and then discovered that those who made them were indeed in earnest.

One night as he was about to fall asleep, the phone rang. An angry voice said, "Listen, nigger, we've taken all we want from you. Before next week you'll be sorry you ever came to Montgomery."

He hung up but could not sleep. In telling about it later he said, "It seemed that all my fears had come down on me at once. I had reached the saturation point."

He describes his situation in these words: "I got out of bed and began to walk the floor. Finally I went to the kitchen and heated a pot of coffee. I was ready to give up. I tried to think of a way to move out of the picture without appearing to be a coward. In this state of exhaustion, when my courage was almost gone, I determined to take my problem to God. My head in my hands, I bowed over the kitchen table and prayed aloud.

"The words I spoke to God that midnight are still vivid in my memory. 'I am here taking a stand for what I believe is right. But now I am afraid. The people are looking to me for leadership, and if I stand before them without strength and courage, they too will falter. I am at the end of my powers. I have nothing left. I've come to the point where I can't face it alone.'"

At that moment, he tells us, he experienced the presence of God as never before. "It seemed as though I could hear the quiet assurance of an inner voice saying, 'Stand up for righteousness, stand up for truth. God will be at your side forever.' Almost at once my fears began to pass from me. My uncertainty disappeared. I was ready to face anything. The outer situation remained the same, but God had given me inner calm."

Three days later when his home was bombed the inner calmness was still there. In thinking back on this experience later he said, "When our nights become darker than a thousand midnights, let us remember that there is a great benign Power in the universe whose name is God. . . . This is our hope. . . . This is our mandate for seeking to make a better world."*

*Martin Luther King, Jr., *The Strength to Love* (Cleveland: Collins, 1963), pp. 113, 114.

5
Courage

The experience of Martin Luther King, Jr., in the previous chapter clearly illustrates the close connection between serenity and courage. His actions brought him face to face with fear, and he needed serenity, peace within, courage, and strength to go on.

In considering the Serenity Prayer, it is useful to be aware that courage — while not mentioned in the title of the prayer — is central to its meaning.

Serenity is mentioned first in the prayer, so it is used as a convenient label for the prayer as a whole. In fact, the prayer could equally be called the Courage Prayer and the Wisdom Prayer. If the prayer did not include the sections on courage and wisdom, it would express a vastly different attitude toward life as a whole.

While serenity implies a certain peacefulness, praying for courage to change has an uneasiness about it. Not that I would not like to think of myself as a courageous person; I just associate courage with a danger of some sort. Courage has an unsafe side that is disturbing.

You may have had an experience similar to mine as the prayer moves away from the subject of serenity and toward courage. Almost without realizing it, we can drift into the automatic replay in which we repeat words without much thought about their meaning.

Yet avoiding this section of the prayer about courage greatly changes its meaning. One of the reasons the prayer is so popular is its realism. Instead of associating God with an otherworldly approach to life or an escape of some sort, the prayer emphasizes moving into life, not away from it.

To pray for "courage to change" is to participate in a particular viewpoint about life, a viewpoint that also says something vital both about God's relationship to the world and about ourselves as human beings.

It is important to underscore what the prayer is *not* saying. It does not say that all the problems of the world are unreal, that if we just looked at the difficulties we face from another viewpoint we would see that all is well, that our problems are simply an illusion.

This prayer is clearly saying something else — that there are changes to be made, that God's will is not being done on earth, and that we need strength and a vision within us to make those changes come about.

A lot of people have difficulty thinking about a world in which God's will is not always being done. In the midst of tragedy some people find comfort in saying, "I don't understand it, but it is God's will that it happened. It is for our learning about life."

I find it very difficult to accept that some of the horrors in the world take place simply to test us or teach us something. Every automobile accident is God's will? People abusing and torturing others somehow makes sense? One person callously ridiculing another is all right if seen from God's point of view? To say that such painful situations are all just lessons is, for me, straining belief in God beyond the breaking point.

The author of this prayer, as we will see later (in the chapter on wisdom), looks at God and the human situation quite differently. Instead of everything being God's will he sees that most of the problems we face are the result of human beings' misuse of freedom.

While God has created a basically good and reliable world, it is now a fallen world. It is a world that has fallen below what it is intended to be because of human foolishness, and it needs to be repaired.

To have courage to change is to recognize that things have gone wrong because of what we and others have done and that we need the strength that comes from God to set things straight.

While the actual words here are "to change the things I can," the basic meaning behind these words seems to imply something more. The object is not simply to change whatever I can — whatever I'm able to change — but instead "to change the things I can" *that need to be changed.*

The original prayer, in fact, used the words "courage to change *what should be changed.*"

Unfortunately, the word *should* today has come to have a negative meaning for some people. A friend of mine says he cannot stand the word *should* because it affects him so strongly emotionally. More than once I have heard people express, with great feeling, "There are no 'shoulds'!"

It is understandable that those who have grown up in dysfunctional families — where *should* was constantly used to create pressure and guilt — would find the word distasteful. But another use of the word *should* helps to make sense of this part of the prayer. To change what should be changed is to get things to be what they are intended to be — to look at the world and to see what needs to be done and to make repairs.

In the Twelve-Step program of recovery, one of the steps speaks about developing a conscious contact with God, praying for knowledge of God's will and the power to carry that out. To pray for change is to pray for understanding about what needs to be done and the strength to accomplish it.

To pray for courage, then, does not mean praying for some sort of denial that danger exists. On the contrary, real courage always carries within it an awareness of fear. Situations in which we are completely sure of our safety are not ones that call for acts of courage! To be courageous is to make a decision and act on it when we are afraid.

Courage seems to have two parts: decision and action. While others may sometimes see the act of courage itself, what they often do not see is the other part of courage, the inner struggle that comes before the action.

Because such fear is often hidden within a person, some acts of courage may not appear courageous at all and may, in fact, seem quite ordinary.

I think of Jane, divorced for many months, who after long deliberation decided to attend a group for single people. In telling me about it afterward, she said she had driven her car to an adjoining town, finally reaching the door of the building where the group was meeting.

Then almost immediately she turned her car around and headed back toward home.

When she arrived in her driveway she sat in her car and thought about her life. Then, with fear and trembling, she turned her car around again and headed back toward the meeting. When she walked through the door, few if any saw her presence there as the act of courage that it was.

A hidden part of courage is the inner struggle to become willing to do something we fear. This struggle can sometimes be even more difficult than taking action on what we have decided. In some situations we are hesitant because we are not clear about what to do. In other circumstances, however, we may be very clear about what needs to happen, but we just don't want to do it! Sometimes the problem is not about clarity but about our *becoming willing*.

We may need to ask before we pray, "Am I praying to change something that I don't want to change anyway?"

A recovering alcoholic once told me that before she became sober she used to pray, while she was pouring a drink, "O God, don't let me pour this drink!" Later, when she had stopped drinking, she laughingly spoke about how she had not, at that time, seen anything inconsistent in her prayer.

It seems reasonable to me that God's way is not to invade the human personality and take away our freedom to choose. Such action would mean that the very foundation of human character would be lost. We would be puppets, not people.

To pray for courage is to make a statement about ourselves and our relationship to God's will. It means taking a stand that we want to participate in God's intentions for us and the world.

The strength and courage that result from such a prayer are not, of course, some sort of reward from God for praying in the right way. Instead, the prayer creates a situation that makes receiving possible. It is more like turning on a lamp in a home. The light comes to us not because we deserve a reward for flipping a switch. It is simply the way it is. We have done something that makes receiving possible.

Praying for courage also says something about our understanding of God.

One of the deepest questions we can face is whether there is any meaning behind what we see in the world. Is the whole thing simply some sort of accidental happening, or is there some purpose behind it all? And if there is a purpose, is it good?

To think that we will somehow find complete answers to those questions and never doubt again is unrealistic to life as we know it. Life is an unfolding process in which deepening answers come to us as we live and grow.

But how, then, do we get courage?

On the one hand, it seems that courage grows out of our struggle to understand life. It is the result of values that come from thought and experience. On the other hand, the Serenity Prayer seems to imply that courage is something God gives us when we pray for it. Which is it?

My guess is both.

Courage does seem to come about, at least partly, through human effort. When I hear about a person who is courageous I feel respect for that person — that he or she is in some way responsible for the courage shown. To see the person's courage as simply a gift from God would not seem particularly worthy of admiration.

Something about courage appears to be related to a person's character. Courage is partly the result of an inner struggle that gradually establishes a position or viewpoint about life that has a strength of conviction about it.

Yet it also seems that a part of courage is given. There are times when, in spite of all we have done, thought, and experienced, more is needed. There are times when our convictions do not seem strong enough, when our emotions overwhelm our thinking. There are times when, in spite of all we have done, no matter how hard we try, we become *dis*-couraged.

Surprisingly, it seems that when we reach that

low point we also may experience a change within ourselves that makes us more open to receiving insight and courage.

Jesus said, "Blessed [happy] are the poor in spirit" (Matt. 5:3, KJV). Our first response to these words might be, "Wait a minute! There must be some mistake. Why would he say that? Obviously it's supposed to be the *rich* in spirit, not the poor in spirit, who are happy."

Actually, the turning point when we receive insight and strength is usually not when we are most confident but when we are poor in spirit, when we have a need for a Power greater than ourselves. At the point when we reach the limits of our own thought and experience God provides what we are not able to do for ourselves.

Two parts, then, contribute to courage: what we do, and what God does.

Our part begins through *risking awareness* of something we fear. But to do that requires courage! It sounds like a catch-22 situation (without experience, you can't get the job, but unless you get the job, you can't get experience). It seems that the way to *get* courage is to *have* courage!

Yet this is not quite as difficult and impossible as it at first sounds. Samuel Miller, in his book *The Life of the Soul,* reminds us that such a pattern of growth occurs in other areas of life as well. He says that the only way we can *become* a carpenter is to *be* a carpenter. What he means by this is that by picking up a saw and sawing a piece of wood (being a carpenter) one becomes a carpenter!

In the beginning the quality of the work may be somewhat limited. Yet, strangely, being what we want to be leads to becoming what we want to be.

So also with courage. Taking a small step of courage, though limited, leads on to more courage. Strange as it may seem, we become courageous by being courageous.

But courage is more than simply doing something that we fear. Doing anything just because we are afraid of it could be sheer foolishness. Real courage is holding fast to those values that have deep meaning for us. In fact, the amount of courage we have is directly related to the meaning and significance we give to our lives.

For this reason it is vital to develop a growing understanding of who we are, of what it means to be human beings in this puzzling and complicated world, and of the difference that courage can make in all that happens in our lives.

Playwright Arthur Miller once wrote an article in the *New York Times* in which he told about how he came to write the play *Incident at Vichy*.

The play is based on an incident related to Arthur Miller by a friend. The friend knew a man, a Jew who was picked up in the streets of Vichy, France, in 1942. He was

taken to a police station and simply told to wait in line.
A door to an office at the head of the line would open
from time to time, and persons would be beckoned in one
by one. Some returned, some did not. The rumor came
down the line that this was a Gestapo operation and that
only those who could prove that they were not Jews could
go free. The Jew moved closer and closer to the door until
there was only one man between him and the door. For
him it seemed as though nothing stood between him and
senseless death.

Finally the door opened, and the man who had
been last to go in came out. But as this man, a Gentile,
left on his way to freedom, he stopped in front of the Jew
and quietly handed the Jew his pass. The Jew had never
seen the Gentile before and never saw him again, but he
left that police station a free man.

Arthur Miller tells us that for ten years he thought
about that incident and its meaning for life. He said that
the unknown man who gave away his pass came into
his thoughts many times — as he read of the people in
Queens who failed to call the police when a woman
was stabbed to death in the street below, as he thought
of the plight of the blacks or the destruction of the
Jews in Europe.

He began to see that in this complicated world all
of us are somehow involved in acts of injustice. In one
way or another each one of us is guilty of not standing up

for justice in situations we face, and as a result innocent people are hurt.

Miller tells us that his thoughts turned to three young men who, in the early years of the civil rights movement, were murdered in Mississippi. Why were their lives different from hundreds who had been lynched and beaten to death before them? "The difference, I think," said Miller, "is that these, including Chaney, the young Negro, were not inevitable victims of Mississippi, but volunteers. They had transformed guilt into responsibility, and in so doing opened the way to a vision that leaped the pit of remorse and helplessness."*

One of the values of the Serenity Prayer is that each section of the prayer contributes to and enriches another. To know the meaning of courage is also to know the meaning of wisdom. The final section of the book will shed further light on human nature and our significance as individuals.

Because courage is so closely connected to wisdom you may find it useful to return again to this chapter on courage after reading the chapter on wisdom.

*New York Times, 3 Jan. 1965, Magazine section.

6

To Change the Things I Can

When a crisis occurs, we are reminded that our beliefs about life — though hidden — are always present within, influencing our lives in one way or another. A person who seems strong may not have much inner strength. A person who outwardly appears weak and frail may in fact turn out to have deep courage and insight.

Sarah comes to mind. Married about twenty-five years in a traditional, rather quiet marriage, she came in to see me and told of a disturbing experience that had occurred the previous evening. She and her husband were seated in their living room. He appeared to be deep in thought, and she asked him what was on his mind. He put his head in his hands and began to cry. "I want a divorce," he said. "I'm in love with another woman."

Within a few hours he moved out of the home and did not return.

Suddenly, without warning, Sarah's familiar pattern of living was altered permanently. Painfully she kept going. In spite of the hurt and rejection, she was able to draw on a source of courage and hope within her. In her middle fifties, she began a new life, eventually finding a loving relationship with another man. And, through her courage to change, she found increasing strength in spite of difficult circumstances.

I have given a lot of thought, over a period of years, to the effect viewpoint has in a person's life. I have wondered why some people live primarily with fear and anxiety, while others, in similar circumstances, work through their problems with a quiet inner strength.

I have asked myself, "What's in a belief system that helps people meet difficulties in life with courage and hope?" At first I thought that such people must have strong, unwavering beliefs that remained unchanged no matter what the circumstances. Yet the more I observed people with that special quality of living, the more the opposite seemed to be true. Rather than having fixed, rigid beliefs, I noticed instead *flexibility*.

They showed an openness to new information even when it might change what they believed. Instead of defending their beliefs in some rigid way for their security, they had a basic framework of trust that allowed for adjustments in what they saw as true.

In fact, it seemed that those with the strongest dogmatic beliefs were often the least capable of handling an unexpected tragedy. It was almost as if rigid beliefs were made of some brittle material that shattered under stress, while flexible beliefs bent but still remained strong under the pressure of events.

The more I thought about flexibility the more it seemed to be near the heart of a workable belief system. A central trait of the psychologically healthy person seems to be *a willingness to look at life from another viewpoint — to risk becoming aware of something new.*

Whatever a person's belief system, those best able to meet life's difficulties with courage and hope seem to have an underlying sense of faith or trust in life. While those who have such trust may not experience it continuously, I have noticed that when it is present a person is willing to face a difficult problem and work it through rather than deny the reality of it.

Understandably, at times we all tend to hold onto familiar truths, staying with what has worked well in the past, sometimes at the cost of facing something new that might be unpleasant.

Yesterday I met with a man who, in his fifties, had been fired from his job. He was comparing his attitude toward an employer with that of his son. "My son expects to change jobs often," he told me, "but I'd always had a different attitude toward my work. I told myself that if I'm loyal to the company I work for, they'll be loyal to me." For this man, and at times for all of us, it is painful to discover that the world has changed, that familiar truths are no longer what they once were, that courage to change is needed.

When we experience a profound loss, such as of a job or a loved one, and we can't fit what has happened into a familiar belief system, we may choose one of two routes. Either we will deny what has happened and try to hold onto what has always been true, or we will gradually come to terms with the pain of the situation, slowly make plans for the future, then move on toward something constructive, risking awareness of another kind of world than the one we have known.

Yet even when we are willing to change, it is vital to look carefully at where we are. Different problems can require quite different approaches in solving them.

A helpful first step in bringing about change is often simply to *define the central concern.*

To do this I have found it useful to begin with the question, What type of problem is this?

1. Is it a *practical* problem?
2. Is it a problem with a *relationship*?
3. Or is it a problem *within myself*?

As our answer determines the approach to a solution, it is important to clarify which kind of problem we are facing.

Practical problems are unemotional problems. Practical problems are about "the way things work," without much reference to how people feel about the situation. Figuring out a work plan, improving a time schedule, assembling a piece of equipment, and fixing something that is broken all are practical problems. Practical problems are mainly about changing things or situations in some impersonal way.

Relationship problems have a different emphasis. The central concern is about what happens emotionally between people.

Although such problems may sometimes involve a number of persons, often the concern is about someone in particular. Perhaps there has been a break in a relationship with a person who was once very close. Or we are living with someone who is constantly critical. Or we feel a silent rejection from a person we love. A relationship problem is primarily about a personal, emotional problem between two individuals or within a group.

Problems *within ourselves* are about problems that are just "there" — feelings within us that complicate our lives. Problems within ourselves may include anxiety or fear or a sexual problem. Perhaps we are concerned about self-worth, or about some other inner feeling that we may or may not want to share with others.

Seldom, however, does any problem remain purely in one of these three main categories. Usually difficulties in one area affect another as well. Yet deciding what is the *central concern in the present situation* is a useful starting point in creating change.

While it is helpful to think through any kind of problem with an awareness of God's intention for us, practical problems often lie more in the thinking and doing areas of life than in the area of trust and prayer. This does not mean, however, that prayer cannot be a key in finding a solution. Sometimes, in periods of quiet, the thoughts about the problem will come together in new and creative ways. Sometimes, after thinking through the various possibilities and praying about them, an insight we had not considered will suddenly come to us, perhaps after a night's sleep, or even in a dream.

While it is valuable to think through the possibilities for change, answers do sometimes just come to mind without much analyzing.

I once heard of a woman whose child was very ill.

The child had a rare blood type, and no blood of that type was available in her area. During a moment of silent prayer the mother suddenly remembered someone she had known years before who had mentioned having the blood type she now needed. She was able to contact the person, and a transfusion was arranged for the child, who eventually recovered.

This story is a reminder of the value of receptive listening in prayer. While we have a tendency to view prayer as speaking to God, insights often come in quietness. Just waiting, being silent, is often the most effective way of praying.

In fact, with practical problems we may find it helpful to play over in our minds various possible solutions and check out which solution gives us the most peaceful feeling within. If possible, it is useful to check out that peaceful feeling over a period of days to see if it keeps growing.

We prepare the way for solutions by asking questions about what the central concern is, when it needs to be solved, what limits we face (which realities probably won't change), and what resources are available for help.

Even after much thought and prayer the answer may still not be clear. If it is not, we might ask, "Is there one clear step that we could take that leads in a positive direction?"

Psalm 119 speaks of God's word as a lamp to our feet. "Thy word is a lamp to guide my feet and a light on my path" (Psalm 119:105, NEB). Such a lamp may show us only one step, but as we take that step we often find that a next step becomes clearer.

While defining the heart of the difficulty is helpful in solving practical problems, in problems of relationships or problems within ourselves, finding the cause of the problem is often very difficult.

Relationship problems, for example, often have a quality of hiddenness because we are not always clear about what is happening within the other person. And if we do not know what is wrong — what needs to be changed — we may become frustrated and try to force the other person to make changes, not realizing that such forcing often creates further problems in the relationship.

Under such circumstances, one of the best things we can do is pray *for* the other person — not that our own will be done in the life of the other person, but instead that good may come into his or her life so that that other person will be happier. A man once said that one of the most convincing experiences of the value of prayer is what results when he prays for a person he doesn't like.

In prayer we are seeking God's help in making a situation better. The answer that comes, then, will ultimately be consistent with God's love. To ask God for

something contrary to God's will is inconsistent with any rational understanding of prayer.

One of the ways that the scientific approach to the world has been useful is that it has helped provide a basic framework of understanding for many areas of life. The method of science is to make clear "what is" — to describe what is real. And once we define "what is," we have reached a starting point for both thinking and praying.

Yet while defining "what is" is valuable for both thought and prayer, it is important to note that some things are a lot easier to define than others.

Consider, for example, how to explain what is real in each of the following examples:

   a block of wood
   a painting
   a friend's picture
   a valentine for you
   a loving relationship

It is far easier to describe fully things in this list that are least personal (at the beginning), while it is increasingly difficult to describe or explain things that are most personal (as we move deeper into the list).

Sometimes people complain that talking about spiritual things is "not real." "How real can it be if you can't explain it?"

We need to keep in mind that *the most important things in life are often the most difficult to describe.*

To look at what we see most clearly and assume that what is clear is "most real" is like the drunk who, in the dark of night, dropped his car keys and searched for them a block away — under a street light — because there was more light there! The place that is clearest is not necessarily the place of greatest reality.

Because science has been tremendously successful in making changes in our world we tend to assume that the best way to bring about changes is to use that method — to figure out "what is" and take action.

The scientific approach to problems is most effective in areas of life that are easily defined, such as practical problems, which we can observe directly. Through such observations we have made great progress in improving both the length and the quality of life in a wide variety of ways.

The scientific method of thought and action, however, has been far less effective in dealing with relationships. As a matter of fact, from my experience, it seems that those who primarily look at life objectively often (not always!) have more than their share of problems in home situations. Trying objectively to "make things happen" so that family relationships will improve is frequently a major cause of tension.

Another area where thinking has limited effectiveness is in addressing problems within ourselves. We say such things as, "I think I understand the reason, but I'm continually feeling anxious, and I don't know how to change it."

It is a whole lot easier to take action to change things or situations than it is to change emotions. How then do we go about it? Here psychological discoveries can be of some help.

Science, in spite of its limitations, has been effective in providing knowledge about what happens within us. Not only has science given us medical knowledge — an understanding of how the body operates physically — we now have a good understanding of how the mind functions in handling our thoughts and emotions.

Of all the things we have learned about the human mind, one of the most valuable is our understanding of what is now known in psychology as repression. Understanding repression and how it operates not only is useful in knowing about ourselves, but also is helpful in understanding others and our relationships with them.

Repression is what happens within the mind when we suddenly face a painful or tragic situation in life such as the loss of a job or the death of a friend. Often our first response is, "I just can't believe it's true!"

An automatic reaction takes place within us when

something unexpected and hurtful occurs. The shock of the situation causes the mind to operate on two different levels. On one level we are quite aware that the event actually happened, yet on another level we deny the reality of it.

I believe that God has given us the mental mechanism of repression to help us through the intense pain that is present when we face the shock of a hurtful event.

Repression could be compared to what happens in the human eye when we suddenly face a glaring light, such as when we move out of a dark theater into bright sunlight. As light falls on the iris of the eye, the opening in the eye gets smaller automatically, protecting us from the intensity of light.

In such a situation it is difficult, for a moment, to see clearly. Then, as our eyes adjust to the new surroundings, we see more and more details in the scene before us. After a brief period of temporary blindness, what we could not see before becomes clear.

When a tragic event occurs, repression protects us from seeing what is clearly before us so that we are not overwhelmed by taking in more than we can handle all at once.

Repression cuts down the intensity of surrounding emotional problems. When we are suddenly confronted by a lot of emotional pain, repression reduces the amount so the mind has limited awareness.

It is important to understand, however, that the purpose of repression is usually to give us *temporary* relief — to give us time to adjust to a new situation. Problems arise when, out of anxiety, we close our eyes to reality and continuously deny what now needs to be faced.

It is at this crucial point that faith and trust become the determining factors in bringing about change.

While in solving practical problems the solution often comes through *understanding what is* and *making it happen,* with emotional and spiritual problems more often the solution comes through *accepting what is* and *letting it happen.*

Carl Jung used the term *shadow* to describe that part of us that we do not want. All of us have parts of ourselves that we wish to disown, parts of ourselves that we find difficult to face.

The way out of emotional problems is to recognize that *accepting whatever we feel transforms us.*

Psychologist Carl Rogers has put it this way: "We cannot change, we cannot move away from what we are, until we thoroughly *accept* what we are. Then change seems to come about almost unnoticed."*

---

*Carl Rogers, *On Becoming a Person* (Boston: Houghton Mifflin, 1961), p. 17.

To accept a feeling in this way, however, does not mean that it is all right to *act* on whatever we feel. Such actions can be the essence of immaturity.

We instead can say to ourselves, "It's OK to feel whatever I'm feeling. I don't have to act on it. If I name that feeling — even to myself — and accept it as all right to have, I'll become a more whole person."

Understanding repression in this way not only helps in changing within ourselves, it also can help change our relationships with others. One of the greatest complications that arises when we continuously repress our feelings (refusing to face who we are) is the tendency to project onto other people the very feelings we deny within ourselves. Just as a motion picture projector takes film images and projects them outward onto a screen, we human beings may project the emotions that we deny within ourselves outward and onto other people.

Take anger as an example. If, instead of seeing anger as a healthy and normal response to being threatened, we see it as something bad, we will reject it and project it onto another person or group. What we deny within ourselves we then see "out there."

What happens is something like this: We experience an angry feeling. We may then deny that it is our own anger if we consider anger to be wrong. But if we feel anger is present, it must be coming from somewhere —

probably from the other person, not ourselves. Without being aware of it we then project onto another person the feelings we deny within ourselves.

The root of most relationship problems is not the refusal to obey certain rules but the refusal to face our own shadow — those emotions within that we see as unworthy of us. Without knowing it we project onto others what we refuse to face in ourselves. "You're angry!" "You're oversexed!" "You're weak!"

The more strongly we try to avoid emotions we have disowned within ourselves the more likely we are to project those traits onto another person, and thus prevent the change that is needed within ourselves.

In fact, one of the best ways to discover our own shadow is to be aware of what bothers us most in another person. Very often, if we look at what we most strongly dislike in others, we will find an exaggeration of something we are denying within ourselves.

Unfortunately, instead of risking awareness of ourselves — accepting our own character defects — we create relationship problems by denying unpleasant feelings and then self-righteously putting down the other person as the owner of what we have denied within ourselves.

How then can we deal with those elusive problems within that so deeply affect both our relationships and ourselves?

The central problem here is *denial.*
And the opposite of denial is *faith.*

Denial says, "I must block out — not see — certain
areas of life because those areas make me feel afraid or
depressed or unworthy."

Faith, in contrast, is not naive optimism but rather
*living in the world with both an awareness of reality and trust
in God.* Faith says that while I am sometimes afraid and
depressed, I am optimistic about myself because I am the
creation of an intelligent and caring Higher Power.

In contrast to denial, faith sees the world as basically reliable and good. Faith says, "While I see problems
in the world out there, they are primarily the result of the
gift of human freedom that is misused. And I trust in
God who is continually moving me toward healing —
physically, mentally, emotionally, and spiritually, if I
want it, and sometimes even beyond my acceptance and
awareness.

Faith lives in many people who don't see themselves
as religious yet who trust reliable laws in the natural
world and in the workings of the human mind. People of
faith are willing to take risks in life based on dependable
psychological laws such as, "Facing what I fear in myself
is a healthy thing to do."

A deeper faith, however, sees more subtleties and
shades of meaning in life. Instead of trust based on how

{ 66 }

things work, a person of deep faith understands that values, including such qualities as justice, love, and forgiveness, are ultimately rooted in a basic goodness at the heart of life. Such faith is based in belief in a Higher Power continually operating to bring about what is best for us as individuals in a complicated world.

Changes come about, then, in two different ways:

1. by making it happen
2. by letting it happen

Usually when we think about the words *I can,* our emphasis is on making it happen. Experiencing the words *I can* brings energy to a situation: "I am able to do something about this!" It is exhilarating to know that no matter how unmanageable a problem may be, some sort of action can change things.

Often such a sense of enthusiasm comes with taking action that we may forget that changes can also come about, not through making it happen, but by letting it happen. At times we may not see that taking action to bring about changes can actually hinder the very change we want!

I believe it was Peter Marshall, who at one time was chaplain to the U.S. Senate, who told of a young boy bringing a jumbled fishline to his father to untangle. Each time the father began to make progress, the child reached his fingers into the loosening knots to help — to make it happen sooner. Gently the father kept removing the little hands until the young child came to see that the way to solving the problem was not making it happen but letting it happen.

While practical problems are solved primarily through doing, personal problems are very often solved by letting be — allowing something to happen.

If I could select the one thing from my experience as a family therapist that would most easily change a relationship it would be: *not trying to change the other person.* Respecting the other person's be-ing by listening, really listening, to what is said without giving unwanted advice or criticism does wonders for a relationship. This kind of letting it happen means letting the other person be who he or she is *emotionally.* It does not mean giving blanket permission to do anything, however. It includes giving information (but not advice) about anything that is causing us difficulty: "I'm bothered by . . ." "I'm concerned about . . ." and, if necessary, explaining what needs to be done if it continues. The key here is *quietly* expressing to the other person what is happening within us, and also demonstrating understanding by reflecting back the other person's viewpoint in our own words. *

One way of getting clearer about what God does

---

*For further information about this, see my book *Human Be-ing: How to Have a Creative Relationship Instead of a Power Struggle* (New York: New American Library, 1975).

and what we do in the healing process is to consider our part in physical healing. A cut in the skin heals with minimal effort on our part. All we need to do is keep the wound clean and perhaps apply an antiseptic.

The more we move toward emotional and spiritual healing, however, the more it seems that our willingness is a vital part of the total process.

It appears that God does not automatically change the personality, even for the better, without our permission. Evidently, God does not want to take away our responsibility for doing those things that we need to do for ourselves to promote growth in character.

Enabling is a word frequently used by those participating in recovery programs concerned about dependency. Understanding enabling not only provides direction for us in our relationships with others, it also reminds us that while God helps us, God does not enable us in destructive ways.

In human relationships enabling means taking responsibility for someone else — doing those things that a person should be doing for himself or herself. While seemingly helpful, enabling is ultimately destructive because it gives the one receiving it a distorted view of reality.

A man drinks too much, comes home, throws up in the hall, and falls to the floor in a stupor. The enabling wife struggles to get him on his feet, pulls him up the

stairs, cleans him up, gets him into his pajamas. As he
falls asleep she returns to the hallway, cleans up, and
then, in a state of exhaustion, she returns to bed herself.

At first glance it seems that this is, indeed, a very
loving thing to do. Unfortunately the wife does not real-
ize that her actions are actually helping — enabling — the
husband to keep drinking.

To take away another person's responsibility for
what he or she has done is not ultimately as caring as it
first seems. Keeping a person away from the consequences
of his or her actions adds to denial and gives the person a
false sense of reality.

To wake up in a clean bed instead of sleeping all night
with his face in vomit "enables" a person to keep drinking.

Sometimes the most loving thing we can do for another person is to allow that person to see the consequences of his or her actions. Not protecting, not aiding
in a person's denial may be the very thing that is needed
to prevent further destruction to themselves and others.

We may need to reevaluate what we mean when we
speak of doing what is loving. To do something for someone that the person needs to do for his or her own growth
(even if it makes the *giver* feel better!) is not necessarily a
loving act.

To build muscles we need to push against obstacles
of some sort, such as weights. If a friend wants to help by
lifting a weight with us so that it is easier, she or he

hinders our growth. The same thing can also occur in character growth. Too much helping from another person can be destructive to what we are and what we can become. Making things happen can often be far less helpful than letting things happen.

It is sometimes difficult to know the difference between doing something that is truly caring and doing something that is destructively enabling. Under such circumstances it is useful to ask, "Does this action show respect to *both* myself and the other person?"

Thinking through what it means to do what is loving is valuable in that it helps us clarify what we may expect from God. At times we want God to enable us toward something that will eventually be harmful to ourselves or others. Such enabling would, of course, be contrary to God's love.

Sometimes when God does not enable us in getting something we want, we may think it is a lack of God's love. At those times we need to see the present situation not in isolation but in relationship to other events in our lives. We may gain a deeper perspective by looking back at the past for insight. Someone once compared God's guidance to the experience of being on a boat in a broad expanse of water. By looking ahead it is difficult to tell where we are headed, but by looking back at the wake of the ship we get a sense of direction by seeing where we have been.

$\{\,71\,\}$

In looking back at my life I see events that were quite difficult but that looked far more positive later than they appeared at the time.

As we consider changes in relationships and within ourselves, there seem to be two central keys to change: *acceptance* and *prayer.*

Acceptance can come both from others and from ourselves.

Acceptance by others prepares the way for us to look at ourselves honestly, without denial. When someone accepts us we tend to feel, "If they see me the way I am and they still accept me, maybe I am OK."

Such acceptance usually comes from persons who are honest with themselves and who are also caring listeners. For those in support groups it could be a sponsor who has "been there" and understands in a special way.

While many hesitate to go to professionals to discuss their problems, many professionals are kind and caring and can provide insights that an untrained person does not have. It may be necessary to meet with various people to find the person who is best for you.

Acceptance of ourselves is a continuing process, and while such growth can sometimes be difficult, it can also be exciting. A recovering alcoholic once told me, "I'm moving on from recovery into discovery."

Accepting ourselves means recognizing that all feelings, no matter what they are, are all right to own (but not act on!). Accepting feelings within ourselves is a means to healing.

A crucial step toward accepting feelings includes the naming of our feelings by others or ourselves. Finding a word or phrase to describe a feeling moves us increasingly toward health. Faith in the underlying goodness of creation and the process of continual healing within us helps make such naming of feelings possible.

Prayer is also a vital part of healing in the personal areas of life. Prayer means bringing ourselves to God with a willingness to do those things that are ultimately best for both ourselves and others.

Just as a person might bring a special kind of wood to a cabinetmaker so that the cabinetmaker could design and create a unique piece of furniture, so also God works on the "material" we bring and refines it as we pray.

The material we bring is the information we have gathered and the various alternatives as we see them. While at first this process may seem like simply thinking about the problem and not praying, careful thought is in fact closely related to prayer. Part of the praying process is to think through what needs to be done in light of what we see as God's will for the situation.

A woman who is in recovery from alcohol, heroin, and cocaine addiction once told me that when she finds herself beginning to romance those things that are destructive for her she immediately turns to prayer. To "romance" means to keep paying attention in order to bring something or someone into our lives. Prayer is turning the mind and heart toward those qualities that God would ultimately want us to have for our own good.

One brief concluding note about having a practical approach to change: It is important in making changes to "keep it simple."

I keep asking the question, "What's the simplest way of solving this problem?" *Sometimes it is far better to accept a less than perfect solution than to continuously analyze, waiting for the perfect answer.* I encourage people to keep a balance between a more complete solution and the one that reduces the pain now. We sometimes have a vision of "the way it ought to be," and we pursue the perfect solution instead of solving the problem on a less than perfect level and moving ahead with daily life.

Although circumstantial solutions may not be as complete or lasting as those explored in greater depth, a more superficial solution can sometimes be the best solution. A rather simple example comes from my own life. Under certain circumstances I have an inappropriate and neurotic fear of birds. Generally I am not bothered by them when I am out of doors and they are flying around or nearby. What does frighten me is when I am in some sort of enclosed area with a bird. I think I know where my fear comes from. When I was a child my grandmother had a parakeet. When our family visited her she would open its cage and it would fly around the room, sometimes lighting on her head or shoulder. The prospect of the bird landing on me with those sharp claws made me very uneasy, to say the least.

Even though I know intellectually that this is probably the source of my fear, the problem still affects me emotionally. I remember once being in a caged area in a zoo with birds and hearing my children laughingly call, "Look at Dad!" as I put my hands on my head to protect myself.

While it would be possible to explore my fears further in this area and get cured of my irrational neurotic attitude, I have chosen to solve it instead by turning it into a practical problem. I will simply not put myself in circumstances where I am enclosed in an area with a bird. It is not worth my time and effort to solve the problem in a deeper way psychologically.

If I were working in a zoo or frequently faced situations where this problem had a strong effect on my life, I would work for a more complete solution. As it is, I will just change circumstances and solve my problem that way. Knowing I'm neurotic in that area, I'll just live with it.

While some might consider such an approach denial, some problems in life are more worthy of time than others. To recognize that we are limited creatures with limited choices is part of wisdom.

A discussion of courage and change would be incomplete without emphasizing a central concern of Reinhold Niebuhr — the need for courage and change within groups and organizations. Niebuhr saw organizations as being much more corrupt than the individuals within them.

In his book *Moral Man and Immoral Society,* he tells us, "In every human group there is less reason to guide and check impulse, less capacity for self-transcendence, less ability to comprehend the needs of others and therefore more unrestrained egoism than the individuals, who compose the group, reveal in their personal relationships."*

Practical experience seems to confirm this in many ways. In organizations we often hear comments such as these: "It's not my area of concern" or "It's just company policy" or "We can't make any exceptions."

Niebuhr points out that we can, without realizing it, use an organization to cloud responsibility and do things we would never do in face-to-face situations.

For Niebuhr, to care for persons does not simply mean loving those close to us, but creating change in

---

*Reinhold Niebuhr, *Moral Man and Immoral Society* (New York: Scribner, 1952), p. xi.

those impersonal areas of decision where an organization or system harms or dehumanizes individuals.

From this perspective, a spiritual person is not one who lives apart from the world to maintain personal purity or to find serenity, but instead, one who takes responsibility for healing in a broken world.

Sometimes seemingly impersonal decisions can profoundly affect the lives of many people. Niebuhr challenges each of us to look carefully at the particular organization of which we are a part and raise questions about the ultimate effect of the system on the lives of individuals who are not part of the decision-making process.

While it is often difficult to make changes in a personal relationship or within ourselves, in an organization or system there is a special need for the insight and strength that comes from praying for the courage to change.

7

Wisdom to Know the Difference

Probably all of us, at one time or another, have asked that most important question in life: "What is it all about?" In simple terms, wisdom means finding an increasingly satisfying answer to that basic query as we face life's difficulties and joys.

We know, of course, that finding what life is all about cannot mean understanding all that can possibly be known. When we say that a person knows all about something — "all about cars" or "all about music" — it does not mean that the person can learn nothing more in those areas. We mean rather that a person has a wider viewpoint — an overall sense of things — instead of just some isolated facts here and there.

To know what life is all about is to have a perspective that fits the details into an overall picture that makes sense, a viewpoint that helps in putting things together.

Developing such a perspective is, of course, a continuing process. While sometimes the answer to a problem is immediately clear, at other times all we can do is find a path that we hope will lead to an answer. *We find answers as we become part of a process.*

Consider the ordinary example of solving a jigsaw puzzle. Much like life, a puzzle has many pieces or parts that need to be fitted together to make sense of the whole picture.

Consider what we do in such circumstances.

If hundreds of pieces of a puzzle are lying on a table before us, one thing we *don't* do is keep picking up two pieces at random to see if they fit with each other. That's the hard way!

We begin to make progress, however, if we
(1) assume the puzzle has some meaning, and
(2) act as if it does.

At the beginning we may have only the vaguest impression of what the final result will be — a picture of some sort with a fixed boundary — yet that is all we need to begin.

With only this limited guess about the meaning, we can start by searching for pieces with straight edges and forming a border, and we can look for pieces with the same color and group them together. By repeatedly returning to these two basic reference points of boundary and color, we find increasing understanding of the overall picture.

While the reference points, as we use them, can still be incomplete in themselves, their value is confirmed by how helpful they are in causing the various parts of the puzzle to fall into place.

Even if we have no proof at the start that the final result will have some sort of meaning, *if we simply guess about that meaning and take action on that basis, we often find that what was uncertain becomes a lot clearer.*

While life itself is far more complicated than a jigsaw puzzle, a similar process of discovery can occur in life as well. Many people have found that by assuming life has meaning and *acting as if* it does, many things that were once puzzling become clearer.

But what reference points can we use as a basis for understanding life itself?

While others may also be of value, these two seem to lead to increasing clarity:

1. understanding ourselves
2. trusting in God

Deepening our understanding of these two areas of life is especially relevant as we seek wisdom to know what

we can and cannot change — what we can do and what
God is doing.

UNDERSTANDING OURSELVES

Understanding ourselves means knowing who we
are both as individuals and as human beings.

Coming to an understanding of who we are as individuals is a very personal process and requires individual
help. Everyone lives with certain patterns from his or her
past that need to be worked through with a caring person, within a supportive group, or through reading in the
special area of concern.

What follows is less specific. It is more of a general
framework — a structure within which individual problems can be considered. It is about an understanding of
ourselves as human beings.

Thinking about who we are as human beings may at
first seem somewhat abstract — perhaps interesting to discuss in philosophical moments with friends, but not particularly relevant to daily living.

Yet almost without realizing it, we all have reached
certain conclusions about our human nature, conclusions
that in subtle and not so subtle ways greatly affect how we
relate to others.

We may be pessimistic about people or cautious or
cynical or optimistic and trusting. But whatever we think

about how people are seems to have a profound effect in our lives. Our overall view of ourselves and others stirs up emotions that determine what we do in a great variety of situations. That overall viewpoint repeatedly affects many areas of our lives.

We may find it difficult, however, to hold any one clear reference point about what people are like. Once we take a position of any sort, an event may occur that causes us to question what we believe. Even the person who is optimistic about everyone may sooner or later become deeply disappointed that someone did not live up to what was expected.

Some feel that the best way to handle situations with people is not to have any expectations, to be basically pessimistic about human goodness in order not to be disappointed.

Yet somehow for me — and perhaps for most people — to see humans as basically bad does not seem quite right. Another side of human beings includes sensitivity, trust, and kindness.

Perhaps we are closer to reality if our reference point for human beings is to see people as basically good. To many, the way to a better world is to have a basic optimism about human nature.

But somehow, as we look at the world today, the answer of optimism about human nature does not quite fit with reality. While we may not want to accept pessimism as a way of life, a hard look at the problems around us makes us hesitate to buy optimism about human nature as a way out of our dilemma. It seems vague and superficial in light of the facts.

Unfortunately, many people have never found a satisfactory answer about who we are and so live by certain assumptions that are sometimes useful in daily living and sometimes not.

It seems that neither the optimistic nor the pessimistic view alone fully squares with life as we know it; or if the basic characteristic of human beings is the ability to reason, why hasn't such reasoning created a better world than we now have?

But what is the alternative?

For me, the most satisfying answer to this dilemma comes from the writer of the Serenity Prayer, Reinhold Niebuhr. Niebuhr's practical viewpoint of human nature was especially influential in the life of Martin Luther King, Jr. Niebuhr's insights profoundly affected King's life and his ministry. King spoke of Niebuhr as having "extraordinary insight into human nature, especially the behavior of nations and social groups."*

*Kenneth L. Smith and Ira G. Zepp, Jr., *Search for the Beloved Community* (Valley Forge: Judson Press, 1974), p. 74.

Because Niebuhr uses theological language, some who read this may assume that they already know what he is going to say. Before jumping to conclusions, it is vital first to understand what his viewpoint is and then ask, "Is this viewpoint true to life as I know it?"

A basic reference point for Niebuhr in his understanding of life is that he is *optimistic about people and realistic about sin.*

Sin? *Sin?*

Isn't the church's emphasis on sin a major cause of emotional problems? Isn't such talk psychologically unhealthy? Isn't telling a person that he or she is sinful often a cause of problems instead of a solution?

Most capable psychologists would probably answer yes to the above questions and understandably so, especially when an emphasis on sin continually undermines self-esteem.

Yet to reject Niebuhr's viewpoint because we assume that we already know what he is going to say is to miss his perceptive insights and their practical applications in life.

When Niebuhr uses the word *sin* he is not simply speaking about a definition frequently used by self-appointed moralistic people. Unfortunately, for many today the word *sin* has come to mean the breaking of a strict code of morals, and its use too often is heard as a self-righteous judgment of one person toward another.

{ 84 }

When Niebuhr uses the word *sin* he is speaking about a common human experience, more subtle and more relevant than the breaking of a moralistic code of conduct.

In the original Hebrew and Greek of the Bible, a commonly used word for sin means "to miss the mark," as an archer might miss a target. To sin can mean to fall short of God's intentions for us, to fail to live up to what we see as basically good for our lives, to rebel against God. *To recognize sin in ourselves can mean having the honesty to face our own defects of character instead of living in pretense about ourselves.*

It is here that the biblical view of human beings and contemporary psychology meet on common ground. Both see the central cause of human problems as *the denial of awareness about ourselves.*

Depth psychology has now demonstrated that in order to avoid facing things we do not like about ourselves we pretend that we are something we are not. We rationalize; we find reasons to justify our destructive actions.

To say that discussions of sin in our lives destroy self-esteem is only a partial truth. To deny the reality of our character defects is ultimately far more destructive to ourselves and others.

One of Niebuhr's key concepts is that *those who are most likely to do evil are those who see themselves as righteous.*

Earlier I quoted Niebuhr as saying, "If there were a drunken orgy somewhere, I would bet ten to one a church member was not in it. But if there were a lynching, I would bet ten to one a church member was in it." Those in a lynch mob, whether religious or nonreligious, do not usually see themselves as doing something wrong. They think they are standing up for what is right. Instead of seeing themselves as exploitive or cruel, they view their action as justified under the circumstances.

A lot of people today are offended by the word *sin* because it is often used by those with a holier-than-thou attitude. Niebuhr challenges those in the church to be increasingly honest with themselves about their own sins and character defects. He sees such self-justification as not only within the church, of course, but outside it as well.

While honesty about ourselves may keep us from drifting into self-righteous arrogance, such awareness by itself is not enough. It needs to be balanced with hope — a positive vision within us.

What Niebuhr helps us do is discover a way of seeing people — including ourselves — in a positive light, a view that is still consistent with life as we know it. His viewpoint has a realism that helps explain the seeming contradictions we find in ourselves and in other people. Without whitewashing our human failings he holds a high vision of expanding possibilities within each person.

Briefly, then, Niebuhr is *optimistic about what we can become* but also *realistic about what we are.*

The value of any reference point in fitting things together becomes clear as we make use of it. If, in coming back to a reference point again and again, we find that what has puzzled us makes more and more sense, chances are we are on the right track.

While understanding Niebuhr's viewpoint on human nature requires some effort, it can put in perspective a way of seeing ourselves and others that helps make sense of much that is confusing in human relationships.

Niebuhr suggests that we take a second look at the biblical understanding of human beings and see how well it fits with the human situation as we experience it in life.

Simply put, to be human is to be a *creature* with a *spiritual* dimension.

To be a *creature* is to be a part of the physical creation, to be in a body, to exist in the material world as an animal.

To have a *spiritual* dimension is to exist beyond space and time — what Niebuhr calls the capacity for "self-transcendence," the ability to step outside of our bodies through our imagination and look back at ourselves as part of the physical world.

It is this double nature that we have as humans — limited by a body yet also unlimited in time and space — that explains a great deal that is puzzling about ourselves.

The ability to visualize ourselves in our surroundings seems to be (as far as we know) unique to human beings. The influence that we have had on the earth itself (both good and bad!) comes from this ability to picture ourselves in the world. We not only experience, we also observe ourselves.

Through this ability to look at ourselves in our surroundings we have been able to *create* — to make music, to design buildings, to invent machines. In addition, it also helps us *relate* in a very special way with others, by seeing ourselves in relationships through our imagination.

Yet this kind of awareness, while valuable, creates problems for us. The spiritual side of us observes the self being in a body that is vulnerable to events in the world — accidents, illness, and ultimately death. We are free but also limited.

Sometimes life becomes difficult because such awareness can cause us to feel insecure. We want to escape from our limitations and be truly free.

Yet what may seem like an escape into freedom may not turn out to be what we expected. Obviously those who seek to be free by pretending through drugs, relationships, gambling, or in other ways ultimately find themselves less free.

Someone once described false freedom as what happens to a train when it leaves the narrow limits of the track and runs "freely" across a field. While in one sense it is more free than it was when it was confined to the track, in another sense it is not free at all.

As human beings, like the train *we are most free when we are fulfilling our purpose.* When we try to escape our humanness we ultimately find ourselves not only less human but also less free.

But how do we know if we are trying to escape our humanness? One way we know is that we feel a sense of incompleteness about ourselves, an attitude that something basic is missing in life.

This feeling is usually the result of putting too much emphasis on one area of life to the neglect of another. Most commonly, a sense of incompleteness comes when a person tries to find basic security in material things and neglects the spiritual side of life. Or, on the other hand, something is missing when a person tries to escape the physical world and be only "spiritual," denying the physical side of humanness, which is basically good and intended for our growth and pleasure.

As human beings, then, it seems that we have the capacity both to *experience* and to *observe.* In dealing with changes within us we need a perspective where we are conscious of our self without being self-conscious.

One example of this is our attitude toward sex. Many sexual problems are the result of "leaving the body" and becoming a self-conscious spectator of the experience. In creating change it is helpful to become conscious of our self, in a body that is basically good, fully experiencing what is happening. With some sexual problems, making a conscious effort to move away from being a spectator and toward being an experiencer can be a key to change.

To see our present life as purely spiritual, without a physical dimension, can be as unhealthy as seeing life as only physical and neglecting the spiritual dimension.

Behind the Serenity Prayer is the viewpoint that as human beings we are both physical and spiritual. Seeing ourselves in this way provides an increasingly valuable perspective in understanding the human situation and our world.

For example, we can see that disturbing human actions are not rooted in basic evilness, but in fear — a fear that comes from seeing our limitations. This uneasiness about ourselves causes us to hide feelings of insecurity from both others and ourselves.

One way of hiding is by attempting to become powerful in relation to other people. If we can look down on others and see ourselves as more powerful, we may feel less limited. Common ways of doing this are gaining political power for the prestige that it brings, acquiring wealth as a demonstration of greatness, or seeking fame for the sake of fame itself. More commonly, we criticize others in order to demonstrate our own superiority. Interestingly, in many situations other people see such tactics for what they are. And often the person who is most deceived is the one who is doing the pretending.

Another way of hiding from seeing ourselves is by developing an attachment to someone who seems to have power. Continuously giving in to a powerful person may lead that person to like us enough to share what she or he has and lead us to feeling better, less limited, less anxious.

At times, all of us have used these maneuvers or similar ones to make us feel secure. Although we miss the mark by doing so, it does not mean that those who take such actions are basically bad people. Behind what is done is not a basic tendency to be evil, but fear about self-worth.

Such awareness can help us be more accepting of both others and ourselves. We can be more understanding of another person's character defects if we become aware that behind the other's actions is not basic evil but anxiety about him- or herself.

Such awareness also helps us to be less judgmental of ourselves. If we see our foolish actions originating in our own lack of self-esteem we will be less likely to see ourselves as basically bad.

Although such a viewpoint helps us in being more understanding of others and ourselves, this does not mean that we should naively believe in some Pollyanna way that other people will not be destructive and cruel, or that we will not do the same.

Niebuhr's ideas are particularly useful because he is realistic about sin and character defects in all of us. To broadly label some people as good people and others as bad people is simplistic. Each of us as an individual, when we feel insecure, has the potential within to be destructive. And, as Niebuhr points out, the potential for evil in groups and organizations is even greater than within the individual.

The basic reason for our problems, then, is not that human nature is basically evil, but that out of anxiety — lack of trust — we misuse our freedom.

One part of wisdom, then, is to develop a way of looking at people — including ourselves — that is both optimistic and realistic.

Our optimism is rooted in trust in a Higher Power who has created a basically reliable world for our good. That good includes dependence on laws of nature, freedom to choose, and relationships with one another. These qualities, while making possible the joy of creating and relating, also make destructiveness in human beings a reality.

Neither pessimism nor optimism about people fully fits the human situation as we know it. To trust in humans as basically rational when we see that as humans

we rationalize for our own vested interest is naive,
to say the least.

Part of wisdom is to have a realistic view of human
nature, to recognize our potential as human beings as
well as what we are now. This optimism about who we
are as human beings grows out of an understanding that
the world is basically reliable and good because it has
been created and is sustained by a loving God.

Such trust, then, can also be a vital reference in
living. Understanding what it means to trust in God and
acting on it is another path to growth.

TRUSTING IN GOD

One of the difficulties we face in trusting God is
trusting him when we do not fully understand who he is.

Yet such trusting is not something that just happens
once; it is a continuous growing process that begins before we are entirely sure. Trust grows as we act on the
trust that we already have.

But there are some common barriers we may face
that may cause us to hesitate — unresolved questions that
make us wonder about who God is.

For example, many people have difficulty thinking
of God as personal — a Personal Being of some sort. Part
of the problem here seems to be our natural tendency to

equate personal with human — and even visualizing a
physical body. Yet picturing God, the Creator of the universe, in some physical form seems inconsistent with reality as we know it.

Where would God in human form be located? How
big is God? Is God living beyond the farthest galaxy? If
so, how can I know God?

On the other hand, if God is *the source of all that is
most personal in life,* to think of God in less than personal
terms, as an "it," also seems inconsistent. The problem of
describing God appears to require personal language of
some sort. Yet to speak in personal terms without seeing
God as human is very difficult. Our language is inade-
quate. Yet it seems closer to the reality of God to use
personal words instead of impersonal ones.

A phrase that seems to create problems in thinking
about God is the traditional description of humans as
being made "in God's image." It is difficult to use the
word *image* and not think in visual terms.

Yet in spite of the confusion, the word *image* does
have value for our understanding. To have an image
of something is to have a likeness of something else.
I interpret the words *image of God* as applied to humans to mean that there is a spirit within us that is
like God's Spirit.

One experience of that spirit is found in moments of
inspiration that move us to tears. When a person's noble

actions touch us deep within, we shed a special kind of tears. The tears come not from sadness, but from an understanding of life that has great meaning for us. In its origins, to be inspired has the sense of being "in-spirit." At such times we are in touch with our spiritual nature — at the heart of who we are.

Think of any movie or play you have seen. The turning point of the story is often the point at which someone gains some insight into life that he or she did not have before — a moving away from a limited view of life to a deeper knowledge of what it means to be alive.

At such moments, it seems that there is a resonance with God — much like when one tuning fork vibrates in response to another. Yet our human response is not quite as automatic. It seems to require a willingness to respond. While God is seeking to help us become more fully what we are, it also appears that we are able to rebel against our essential natures, and even then, that God works to bring about good in our lives.

It is almost as if God were like a master chess player playing against a novice. But God, instead of trying to defeat us, is constantly moving the pieces to make it easier for us. Even when we make a wrong move, it seems that God keeps rearranging things to make the next move easier, over and over again in the midst of our mistakes.

While there is a danger of magical thinking in interpreting all events as God's will, God sometimes seems to bring help to us through people in ways that at the time seem to be mere coincidence, as when a helpful person unexpectedly appears and improves the situation.

As an example of this type of coincidence, I recall a time when I was facing a difficult problem with a relationship. I had thought about it and prayed about it, but I still felt unclear. I happened to have a short time between appointments at my office, so I decided to go out for a brief walk. As I walked along I glanced up to see a car stopped at a traffic light. Inside was the one person who knew the most about my problem. I signaled to him, we were able to meet and discuss the situation, and I came to see the problem from a new perspective.

What impresses me about these kinds of coincidences is the exquisite timing required for such events to occur. A few seconds difference for either of us, and we would not have met. While some might interpret this incident as purely an accidental meeting, I find that such situations are not an uncommon experience for many people.*

I don't interpret this as God selecting some persons to help and neglecting others, however. Instead, it seems that at the times when we are most open to God's lead-

*See *Came to Believe* (New York: Alcoholics Anonymous World Services, 1973), pp. 67–75.

ing, we are more likely to put ourselves in situations where something helpful might occur.

However, it doesn't seem reasonable to me that therefore there is a hidden plan for each person in everything that happens. I find it difficult to believe, for instance, that if a plane is late in arriving that there is some special meaning in that event for each individual passenger.

It also seems possible that some things that might be helpful to many people never come about because there is no one present who is open to God's purpose for the situation.

Another problem we might face when thinking about God is God's relationship to ourselves. How could we possibly be of value as individuals in the overall events of the world? We might question our significance to God when we are only one among billions of other people. How individually caring can God be under such circumstances?

Yet on the other hand we experience situations where we are taken care of individually by a Higher Power in a way that has little to do with other events in the world. When we are injured physically, as when a hand is cut or scraped, gradually the cut closes, a scar forms, and the skin is eventually restored similar to what it was originally.

Such healing occurs in an individual way with al-most no effort on the part of the person who is healed. It just happens. Evidently some Higher Power beyond ourselves promotes healing and wholeness in us as individuals.

We now have strong evidence from psychology that such healing occurs not only physically but emotionally as well. Psychological patterns within us move us toward emotional healing and wholeness in much the same way as takes place in physical healing.

Even so, we still face the fact of the seeming insig-nificance of people in a huge universe whose size staggers the imagination. Distances are so great that things are measured in light years — the distance light travels (at 186,000 miles per *second*) in one year. How can people be of value when we are like specks of dust on a planet that is itself a speck of dust in comparison to the rest of the universe?

Part of the problem here is our tendency to see value in terms of size. It sometimes seems that bigger is better. To own a bigger piece of land is better than owning a smaller one. A large house is of more value than a small one, and so on.

Yet it is not always true that something larger is better than something small. A tiny diamond can be worth far more than a rock thousands of times its size and weight.

{ 98 }

A major reason that we see ourselves as so utterly insigificant in the universe is that we have used size as the reference point for value.

Suppose, however, that we shift our viewpoint away from size as the basic measure of significance and instead see complexity as the basic reference point. In this sense a computer chip may be worth far more than a table that is millions of times greater in size and weight.

If we see human beings as of little worth because we are so small, we may need to reexamine the basic reference point by which we measure value.

Eric Chaisson, who received his doctorate in astrophysics from Harvard University, has described the human brain as "the most exquisitely complex clump of matter in the known universe." In his book *The Life Era* he compares the complexity of the human brain with that of animals, plants, and even stars. He uses the term *flux density* to describe the quantity of energy emitted per unit of time through a unit of surface area. He tells us, "Though the flux of energy through a star is obviously hugely larger than through our human bodies or brains, the flux *densities* are much larger for the latter."*

Chaisson says that in this sense plants and animals are far more complex than the sun and that the human

*Eric Chaisson, *The Life Era* (New York: Norton, 1989), pp. 253, 254.

brain, for its size, is 150,000 times more complex than the Milky Way galaxy!

In terms of value per square inch, then, human beings far surpass anything else we know in regard to quality and uniqueness. If we measure value not simply in terms of size alone, but in terms of complexity, then human beings can be seen as of profound significance in the universe!

If we were to imagine ourselves in outer space looking at the tiny planet earth, a tremendously powerful telescope would not reveal a single human form in the telescopic image. Humans would be insignificant. But suppose we used another standard for significance, not size but complexity. We would find not one but millions and millions of that unit which is "the most exquisitely complex clump of matter in the known universe." Under such conditions each human being would be both unique and significant.

Or imagine a radio station broadcasting into an area containing five hundred thousand portable radios. Such an area would be seen by the radio station as of far greater value than hundreds of miles of mountain range without a radio. While radios are a less than perfect analogy for those receiving units we call human beings, thinking in such terms is one more way of shifting our understanding of value away from size and toward complexity.

{ 100 }

This understanding of complexity is, of course, not inconsistent with the phrase "keep it simple." The very complexity of the human mind is what gives us the capacity to select priorities in life, a capacity that makes it possible to simplify.

Sometimes people are cynical about having any kind of understanding of God. Such people might well consider some thoughts about gaining knowledge from Isaac Asimov, one of the most widely known and respected science writers of our time. Asimov once wrote an article stating that now, finally, we have a good understanding of the basic rules of the universe.

One of his readers, a student in English literature, after reading the article wrote a letter to Asimov informing him that he was wrong. After quoting the writing, the student proceeded to lecture Asimov severely, telling him that "in *every* century people have thought they understood the Universe at last, and in *every* century they were proved to be wrong. It follows that the one thing we can say about modern 'knowledge' is that it is *wrong*."*

Asimov responded that he did not agree with the student. Just because we have a good but not perfect understanding of something, it does not automatically fol-

---

*Isaac Asimov, *The Relativity of Wrong* (New York: Windsor, 1989), p. 288.

{ 101 }

low that it is all wrong. Such thinking, he says, comes from teachings in the early grades that give the impression that there is only one absolutely right answer, and that unless you give that one answer you are absolutely wrong.

We need to be aware, says Asimov, that there is also a "relativity of wrong." Some answers are less wrong than others.

For example, Asimov tells us, in answer to the question "How much is 2 + 2?" the answer 3.999 is less wrong than 2 + 2 = 17. And spelling the word *sugar* s–h–u–g–e–r is less wrong than p–q–z–z–f.

Asimov's point is this: When an answer falls short of being completely right, that does not mean that it is absolutely wrong.

Scientists do not constantly replace something that is all wrong with something new that is entirely correct. Instead, they increasingly move toward a better understanding of the subject as a whole.

Asimov puts it this way: "What actually happens is that once scientists get hold of a good concept they gradually refine and extend it with greater subtlety as their instruments of measurement improve. Theories are not so much wrong as incomplete."*

*Ibid., pp. 287–91, 298.

Wisdom is not a constant replacement of wrong answers with right ones. Instead, wisdom means moving closer and closer to a better understanding.

Many people today are concerned that some religious institutions have proclaimed their own viewpoints as absolutely right, criticizing others who do not agree as absolutely wrong. Some holding this narrow-minded viewpoint have, at times, used harsh and extreme measures to force others to agree with their particular brand of truth.

Unfortunately, probably because of the above attitudes, the pendulum has now swung to another extreme. We hear such things as, "People who go to church are hypocrites"; "Organized religion is all wrong"; "Nobody has any idea what God is like."

To speak of religion as either right or wrong is simplistic thinking. In religion, as in science, there is a relativity of wrong. A great many people have given much thought to the experience of God in human life. And such reflection has grown and been refined over centuries. Some views are closer to reality than others. We can enrich ourselves and others by reading the writings of those who have devoted their lives to this area and then evaluating for ourselves.

While it is not possible here to review even briefly the works of such writers, there is one such person in recent years who many have found to be particularly insightful. His name is Pierre Teilhard de Chardin.

Teilhard de Chardin sees the generally accepted view of evolution as a valuable clue in understanding God and knowing ourselves as human beings.

Teilhard de Chardin, a Roman Catholic priest as well as a scientist, was prevented by church authorities from both teaching and publishing his ideas during his lifetime. Yet since his death in 1955, his thoughts have become increasingly influential. While I have a far from complete understanding of all that he has written, I find his perspective on life both hopeful and intellectually stimulating.

He asked the question, What would happen if we were to look at human beings, not culturally or from a traditional religious perspective, but in terms of *evolution*? What would happen if we were to stand outside ourselves and objectively consider the phenomenon, or scientifically observable *fact,* of who we are as human creatures?*

As a paleontologist, Teilhard de Chardin studied plant and animal fossils from various time periods in the life of the earth. As he compared earlier periods with later periods he sensed that living organisms contained

*His best-known book is *The Phenomenon of Man* (New York: Harper and Brothers, 1959).

within themselves a force or tendency that moved them toward increasing complexity.

He saw human beings as being at the leading edge of evolution — the most complex of all that has been created. While all animals seem to have the capacity to think, Teilhard de Chardin sees that another more complex step has occurred in humans.

He sees humans as animals who have reached a new level of evolution through the ability to be reflective. By *reflective* he means "being able to know that we know," to see ourselves as the object of our thought. It means that our thinking is not simply an instinctive response to the world but that we can, as Niebuhr also points out, move beyond our bodies and see ourselves in the world.

The practical consequence of this concept is that it provides an additional perspective on who we are as human beings, and deepens our understanding of God's purpose in moving us toward becoming more truly ourselves through increased awareness.

For Teilhard de Chardin, it seemed that the changes in evolution were not just haphazard occurrences, but a force originating in God with a movement toward life, in the deepest sense of the word, and even more, toward conscious awareness and personality.

With the human capacity to imagine ourselves in time and space has come the ability to create and change many things in our world, and through such increased awareness we are now actually becoming *participants* in the continuing process of evolution.

As humans, we have, through conscious choice, increased the complexity of life on earth in countless ways by creating new things: computers, telephone networks, air travel.

It seems that now, in this present period in history, we may have reached yet another step in evolution, and this time with a different quality than all previous evolutionary steps. Instead of growth occurring within us biologically, as in the past, it seems that now, through our increased awareness, a change is occurring outside of our bodies through human technology.

Teilhard de Chardin saw the next stage of evolution as moving into a new *worldwide interconnection of human beings,* a new whole, a new organism, something more than simply the sum total of the population.

Since Teilhard de Chardin first wrote, this idea has increasingly become a practical reality. Through rapid transportation and communication satellites we are now creating a worldwide network of relationships between people. Our expanded ability to communicate greatly increases the complexity of our world and our personal lives, moving us onward toward a new wholeness for our planet.

Previously, events that occurred in remote parts of the world were never known by most people. Now, in a very short time, a major event can be known around the earth.

With the development of mass communication and the rapidly increasing population of the earth (a sphere with limited space) it seems that we face a new level of complexity that will move us to a new state of existence, a new level of awareness.

Years ago, before the telephone and the ease of travel, each individual had only a limited number of persons available for contact each day. Today we have a very different situation. Through the telephone, the automobile, and air travel, many lives touch many others.

Even a simple change in one person's life can greatly affect the lives of many others. When this complexity affects us personally, it is difficult not to feel frustrated with the world and perhaps angry with God who seemingly made it that way.

Yet in Teilhard de Chardin's viewpoint, we are, at this time in history, facing a new level of complexity that can move us toward a higher level of being — a new state of existence — that challenges us to fulfill our humanness.

Breakthroughs to a new state of being are often preceded by a state of turbulence in which there seems to be a lack of order, as in water that boils before it reaches another state of being as steam. The world is now going through great changes. It is possible to see the seeming disorder as evidence that life has no meaning or purpose.

Yet there is also another viewpoint: that through our increased awareness and closeness we are coming into another state of be-ing.

Such awareness, if we are willing, can move us to be more fully human than ever before in history, because *it is ultimately awareness, not denial, that creates greater humanness.*

Life at an increasingly faster pace has produced stress in more and more lives, and here also we face a decision that has been a continuous theme in this book: Do I choose awareness or denial?

While the way of awareness is far from easy, awareness means that we have more choices, and ultimately more choices mean greater freedom.

Teilhard de Chardin sees the purpose of God, then, as moving us toward the next stage of evolution, moving us toward a new, deeper worldwide interconnection of human beings.

Does this mean that as we become a part of this new greater world we lose our individuality?

Quite the contrary!

Just as the heart, the lungs, the eyes become truly what they are not apart from the body but within it, so as individuals we can become more uniquely ourselves as we grow in awareness and participate in something greater than ourselves.

We have a choice: to see life as having no meaning and selfishly take whatever we can get to survive, or to see the effect of God lovingly acting in both general and personal ways in our world — moving us toward a higher humanness as we risk becoming aware and as we participate in something greater than ourselves.

Central to Teilhard de Chardin's thought — as it is to Niebuhr's — is the relevance of the spirit in our earthly journey. Both see our present spiritual goal not as escaping from the physical world, but as living more deeply and lovingly in it.

To escape into the purely spiritual is not what our life is about. In a full life on earth the spiritual and physical are combined. Each, as it is nurtured, gives both meaning and enjoyment to the other.

There are times when we pause to reflect — to look at ourselves and make decisions about what to do — when we nurture the spiritual part of who we are. But life is also concrete, down to earth. There is a time for paying bills, for sexual love, for home repairs, for playing a musical instrument, for working at a job, for the physical enjoyment of sports or dancing. Life combines reflection and action. To be human is to discover the joy of creating and relating — to be creators, as God is Creator, and to love, as God is love.

We cannot first figure out what life is about and

then move on to living in the right spirit. Life is a lot more untidy than that! Thoughts about life and the living of it are jumbled together. It is not that some people have finally arrived at the place where they have all the answers and others have not. Everyone is in the process of growth. Even the most mature are still working through problems that linger from the past and are sorting out meanings in the present and future.

In the complicated world in which we live, it is easy to get so caught up in the routine of physical living that the spiritual perspective that gives meaning to the physical becomes neglected.

Many people have found that a faith community can be very helpful in spiritual growth. While individual reading and study can be of great value, we also seem to need that which can come only through a sharing and caring community. The experience of others who are also growing and learning can provide both insight and strength.

Among the most effective caring communities are those based on the Twelve Steps of recovery of Alcoholics Anonymous, steps now used by groups to address a variety of problems. Local newspapers usually list information about which groups are available in local areas.

Many people who have been disappointed in traditional religion as a source of spiritual insight have found through such groups much that has been missing in life.

Some in these groups and elsewhere are also finding insight in a religious heritage they had previously discarded. Many are finding there a much deeper source of spiritual understanding than they had first imagined.

While some religious organizations are simply going through traditional rituals with little thought about their meaning, many others are committed to growth and meeting the needs of a broken world.

We may sometimes forget that much that is of value today, including Twelve-Step program groups, had their roots in so-called traditional religion. Alcoholics Anonymous originally grew out of and was nourished through the church. When Bill W., one of the founders of AA, was alone in a hotel in Akron, Ohio, struggling for sobriety, a church bulletin board and phone calls to churches led him to "Dr. Bob" and the founding of AA based on their joint religious heritage.

The church and other religious organizations have indeed made mistakes, but many thoughtful and caring people in mainline churches and other religious organizations are reaching out in literally thousands of ways to provide practical help to others in organizing soup kitchens, shelters for the homeless, and in the founding of many universities and hospitals. Often religious people have been the voice of justice in the midst of overwhelming difficulties.

Pointing to the Inquisition and other horrible

{ 111 }

things people have done in the name of God does not tell the whole story. We can learn much from faithful people who carefully thought through their understanding of God, who have given service to others as a loving expression of their religion. Joining in worship — sharing in hymns and prayers — can be a vital way of deepening our relationship with God.

Sometimes a person may be hesitant to participate in a spiritual community because it uses symbols that seem mysterious and confusing. Yet asking about the meanings of such symbols often can become the shortest path to a deeper understanding.

Exploring a faith community, however, does not mean accepting whatever the authorities say without question. It is vital in any spiritual growth to keep searching for better answers. To protest is actually a very positive action. *Pro* means to be for something; *test* comes from the same root as testify. To protest is to testify for something.

Instead of discarding a religious heritage as wrong, it is important first to understand what it is actually saying, and then to ask questions and raise doubts. As someone once said, "If we keep doubting we may reach the place where we begin to doubt our doubts!"

A couple of years ago I visited the town in New Jersey where I had spent most of my early years. I was surprised to discover that only one store that had been there in my childhood remained open on the main street, and even that store was under new management. I found the churches, however, still present in the same locations. Not only were they not out of business, they had expanded. Thoughtful and caring people found those places of worship sources for life's meaning. While many who were members years ago had died or moved away, others were using those same buildings for inspiration and service to others.

Many religious concepts, like those in science, began with primitive ideas and have grown and been refined over hundreds of years. Such growth in understanding seems worthy of attention. By looking carefully at traditional religious values to discover what they really are, we may see something that we thought we already knew from a new perspective and find deepening insights we never expected were there.

During World War II a group of men found themselves in a Japanese prison camp in Thailand. They worked in heat that reached 120 degrees. Their bodies were stung by gnats and other insects. Their feet were cut and bruised by sharp stones as they cut down branches and cleared the jungle. They dug earth and carried it in boxes and baskets to build a railroad through the jungle. They suffered from thirst, exhaustion, disease, and starvation in the camp that had become a living hell. Escape was next to impossible.

In writing about it afterward, Ernest Gordon, one of the prisoners, described it this way: "Existence had become so miserable, the odds so heavy against us, that nothing mattered except to survive. . . . The weak were trampled underfoot, the sick ignored or resented, the dead forgotten. . . . When a man lay dying we had no word of mercy. When he cried for help we averted our heads. . . . Many had prayed, but only for themselves. Nothing happened. They had sought personal miracles from the Bible — and none had come. . . . We were the forsaken men — forsaken by our families, by our friends, by our government. Now even God left us . . . In time even hate died, giving way to numb black despair."*

Yet into that death camp came a change that could be described as a miracle. It began because one man saw life as something deeper than the horrors they faced. He gave up his own food for a friend who was sick, and he himself died of starvation and exhaustion.

In discussing the man's death, one of the prisoners was reminded of Jesus' words, "This is my commandment, that ye love one another, as I have loved you. Greater love hath no man than this, that a man lay down his life for his friends" (John 15:12, 13 KJV).

As a result of that one man's action others saw that even in that death camp there was another way of look-

*Ernest Gordon, *Through the Valley of the Kwai* (New York: Harper and Brothers, 1962), pp. 74, 75, 78.

ing at life. Another meaning could be found beyond the horrors of their circumstances. They began to organize crews to help one another. They began to study the Bible. In fact, Bibles came to be in such great demand that they could only be loaned out for an hour at a time.

Prisoner Ernest Gordon, who had been an agnostic and later became dean of the chapel at Princeton University, wrote about the experience afterward in these words: "Through our readings and other discussions we came to know Jesus. He was one of us. He would understand our problems because they were the sort of problems he had faced himself. Like us, he often had no place to lay his head, no food for his belly, no friends in high places. . . . We understood the love expressed so supremely in Jesus was God's love — the same love we were experiencing for ourselves . . . In the light of our new understanding the Crucifixion was seen as being of the utmost relevance to our situation. A God who remained indifferent to the plight of his creatures was not a God with whom we could agree. The Crucifixion, however, told us that God was in our midst suffering with us . . . We looked at the Cross and took strength from the knowledge that it gave us, the knowledge that God was in our midst."*

To have serenity, courage, and wisdom is to catch a glimpse of the values that give meaning to life.

*Ibid., pp. 103, 104, 138–140.

Whatever your spiritual orientation, there are values that give depth and meaning to life and call each of us to acts of love for others and our planet. While it is vital to keep giving thought to what we believe, waiting until everything is clear before taking action means missing out on life itself. While insight can lead to action, it is also true that some insight comes only as we take action on what we already know.

When one person acts on what he or she knows of life it touches the spirit of others, and others find something similar within themselves.

Changes occurred in the death camp because one person responded to what he felt in the depth of his being — a spirit within whose ultimate source was a personal and caring Creator we choose to call God.

> *God*
> *Grant me*
> *Serenity*
> *To accept the things I cannot change*
> *Courage*
> *To change the things I can and*
> *Wisdom to know the difference*
> *AMEN.*